SPORTSPERFORMANCE

TRIATHLON
GOING THE DISTANCE

MIKE PLANT
Foreword by SCOTT MOLINA

D1342588

CONTEMPORARY
BOOKS, INC.
CHICAGO ▪ NEW YORK

Published by Contemporary Books, Inc.
180 North Michigan Avenue, Chicago, Illinois 60601
Manufactured in the United States of America
International Standard Book Number: 0-8092-4774-7

Published simultaneously in Canada by Beaverbooks, Ltd.
195 Allstate Parkway, Valleywood Business Park
Markham, Ontario L3R 4T8 Canada

To Gary Clark. If there is anyone who could serve as a more powerful inspiration to a beginning triathlete, I can't begin to imagine who it might be. And to my wife, Cathleen—happy first anniversary.

CONTENTS

FOREWORD

For a sport so young there is a lot of information available on triathlons. There are also a lot of how-to and how-not-to opinions (that's in *my* book) by so-called experts. What Mike does in *Triathlon: Going the Distance* better than in any other publication is give you a good perspective on how to begin an involvement with triathlons. I thoroughly enjoyed it.

I've been doing triathlons for seven years and I'm still learning a great deal year after year. Everyone has his or her own opinion on how to do these things: runners, swimmers, coaches, critics, wives (!), and so on. Mike's been doing triathlons, covering them for the media, and more importantly, observing triathletes since Triathlon Time began. He's talked with the front-, middle-, and back-of-the-packers. That's the kind of experience he gives you here.

With the right start, triathlons can be a meaningful, positive experience. I love the sport and hope you will, too.

Good reading.

Scott Molina

Thanks to Joanne Ernst and Jim Collins, Storey Lamontagne, Drs. Doug Hiller and Mary O'Toole, Ron Smith, and Ron Marcikic for their invaluable technical assistance.

INTRODUCTION

A number of years ago, before the sport of triathlon became popular, long before Joanne Ernst won the Ironman Triathlon and later ended up on the front page of *USA Today* (before there *was* a *USA Today*), before Dave Scott had a signature line of bicycles, and before Scott Tinley had a clothing line, I covered a rather primitive triathlon in San Diego and made the observation that the competitors looked, ah . . . different. I was writing mostly about running at the time, and to me the emaciated bodies of the runners were the norm; the more muscular triathletes looked bulky and strange. There had been a 10K race on the beach just before the triathlon, so the two groups intermingled. The differences were obvious.

The fact is, the triathletes looked a lot *healthier* than the runners. They seemed to have more fun, too. The runners were serious and withdrawn, the triathletes outgoing and friendly, laughing and teasing each other right up to the start of their event.

I remember the first triathlete who came out of the water in that race sitting in the sand struggling to put his dry shoes on his wet feet and being asked if he wanted anything to drink. Fumbling frantically with his laces, he looked up and cracked, "Yeah, how 'bout a gin and tonic?"

I couldn't imagine a runner saying something like that in the middle of a race. I was hooked.

The sport of triathlon moved beyond its humble beginnings quickly, fascinating the media, drawing to it a large following of dedicated overachievers. Hundreds of people were interested just a few years ago; hundreds of thousands—perhaps millions—are interested now. The sport of triathlon has become popular, even glamorous. I took a photograph a couple of years ago that I thought pretty much summed up the state of the sport: a brand-new BMW 320i zipping down the highway in Phoenix with a triathlon bumper sticker on the rear end and a couple of thousand-dollar bikes on the roof.

If there is a sport that epitomizes the "go for it" philosophy of the last decade, triathlon is surely it.

Still, the sport's popularity hasn't translated into widespread knowledge. Even people who *do* triathlons never received much basic information. I'll never forget the woman who sobbed over the phone at me a couple of years ago after I'd informed her that she could not do the swim of a national championship triathlon wearing a life preserver. "But I *qualified* with one!" she moaned. "And I've made my plane reservations and everything." When I suggested she race without her life preserver she grew indignant. "But I'd never make it!" she said.

I felt terrible. Not terrible enough to try to get her into the race, though. And it was a good thing, considering the conditions on the day of the event. She probably would have drowned—life preserver or not.

This book will fill in some of those information gaps. I've had the good fortune to be close to the best people in triathlons almost from the first days. I've watched them race, interviewed them, written about them. I've formed my own opinions. The information that follows is material I've picked up over the years, all gathered together and poured through a filter. Some of it came through, some didn't. I can't guarantee that everything I suggest will work for you, but it worked for somebody, somewhere—guaranteed. The book will definitely give you enough background so that you can talk about the sport without sounding like an idiot. By the time you've read the last page, you should be able to start training for your first race. By the time you've finished your first race, you probably will be ready to read something more sophisticated. I hope so; this is a fascinating sport because it makes comprehensive use of a fascinating piece of machinery: your body. There's a lot to learn, more than any one book can supply.

I've organized things in a way I hope you will find logical. I started with some historical information, then roughed out current information about triathlons in general—the distances and some of the terminology. There's a section in that first chapter where I move step-by-step through a race, to give you an idea how a triathlon actually works. Some basic training and fitness concepts follow; then we go into the three individual sports.

All the elements that apply to one sport have been kept together. That approach seemed to make the most sense because that's the way a triathlon works: one sport at a time. For instance, you'll read about swimming technique and equipment, training and racing, without having to flip back and forth among three chapters.

I've also avoided getting technical whenever possible. At one point in the first draft I spent a good deal of time trying to describe how to climb a hill on a bike while standing out of the seat. I showed it to a friend, who then looked at me as if I were crazy. "Why?" he asked simply.

Why, indeed? I took that part out. My goal here is to supply some solid, basic information, and present it in a way that won't bore you to death. The intricacies of hill climbing are something that you can worry about later—*after* you've been able to get to the top a couple of times without throwing up.

Mike Plant
San Diego, California
November 12, 1986

xi

Triathlons are often set in dramatic locations. Here are runners and cyclists moving in opposite directions with the Chicago skyline in the background. It was taken at the Chicago Bud Light USTS, the world's largest. More than 3,000 triathletes competed in 1986.

1
THE SPORT OF TRIATHLON

Triathlon was born in Southern California in the mid-seventies. Its first years were quiet and humble, and it was only with the advent of the Ironman competition in 1978 that the word began to spread in earnest. Even then it spread slowly. Until 1981 few people not living on the West Coast had even heard of the sport, and even those who had saw it as not much more than an odd wrinkle on the fitness landscape, a bastard sport populated by self-destructive fools.

The perception changed, however, during an explosive 10-month period in 1982. By the end of that year, triathlon had become a widely recognized, firmly established mass-participation sport in all senses of the word, an entire new industry—short on experience but long on potential and enthusiasm.

The year began on February 14, 1982, when Julie Moss collapsed within sight of the finish line at the Ironman triathlon in Hawaii. She lost first place—and much of her dignity—but she crawled right into the hearts of millions of

Julie Moss made "triathlon" a household word by crawling across the finish line of the Ironman in February, 1982. But she was a better athlete than that indicated. This is Moss winning the Malibu Triathlon a little more than a year after her historic collapse.

television viewers. The "agony of defeat" long heralded by ABC-TV's "Wide World of Sports" was redefined in terms of an activity few people outside of California were aware of. Triathlon purists winced, embarrassed by the puke-and-crawl image of Moss's finish. But her loss was the sport's gain. The general public loved it.

In June the United States Triathlon Series (USTS) held its inaugural event in San Diego. The race attracted a capacity crowd of 600 and distributed the first professional prize purse in the sport: a modest $2,000. It was a start, at least. Four more USTS events, all on the West Coast, followed, as did hundreds of new races around the country. By the end of the summer the media had begun referring to the sport of triathlon as a "phenomenon." It had become "The Sport of the Eighties."

In October the second Ironman event of the year was

The first Bud Light USTS race ever was an historic confrontation. Dave Scott blew the field away, but the "Big Four," the men who would rule the sport for years to come, were unveiled. Above, Scott Tinley is in front; he finished third in this race. Scott Molina, who wound up second, is next. It was the first time that Tinley and Molina had raced against each other. The man in the far rear is Mark Allen, racing in his first triathlon. He finished fourth. In the middle of the group is Dale Basescu, who until the beginning of the 1986 season, was also one of the best in the business. (photo by Diane Johnson)

held. The date had been switched permanently to the fall to give triathletes from temperate climates a chance to train through the summer. The race was no longer the property of wild-eyed kooks from Lotusland: all 850 spots on the starting line had been sold out four months before race day, with 45 states and 10 foreign countries represented. Plans

3

for the next Ironman included a set of qualifying proce-
dures and an entry lottery.

In November the first race produced expressly for professional triathletes was held in Malibu, California. It was
poorly produced and was covered only half-heartedly by
NBC television, but it featured a prize purse of $14,000 and
gave some of the athletes a glint of hope that there was,
indeed, money to be made in the sport. Later that same
month the first European triathlon of any significance was
held in Nice, France. The prize purse was $17,600. A
patched-together team of American athletes nearly froze in
the chilly waters of the Mediterranean but still dominated.

Since 1982, millions of triathletes have entered thousands
of triathlons all over the world. Enthusiasm for the sport
runs high in Japan, South America, Australia, New Zea-
land, Canada, Mexico, and Europe. There is even a
glimmer of interest shining behind the Iron Curtain.

But the sport is still new, and you're still liable to get a
blank look and a "Huh?" if you mention the word "triathlon" on a city street in, say, Boston. Even within the sport,
information often seems to come from several conflicting
sources at once. A little basic training is in order:

tri·ath·lon (trī·ath·lon)

The word has recently been added to Webster's dictionary. It
has come to mean any event that involves a combination of
swimming, cycling, and running, with the events usually
done in that order. More generally, triathlon can mean any
competition that involves three sports. Many of these are
most likely to happen when the weather is extreme. Triathlons that substitute cross-country skiing for the swim are
relatively common. Some throw in paddling a canoe or
rowing a boat. There are people who say that John E. Du
Pont, of the chemical-company Du Ponts, deserves recognition for bringing the sport of triathlon to this country
during the 1960s—in the form of an event that combined
shooting, swimming, and running. The claim is obscure at

best, but it's an interesting footnote. Can you imagine a thousand fools with pistols on the beach in Kona, Hawaii? What would they call it, the Leadman?

IS THE ORDER OF THE THREE EVENTS IMPORTANT?

Yes and no. Safety is one reason for the swim being first. A large group of even well-trained cyclists starting at the same time is dangerous; several hundred relative novices, as would be the case in most triathlons, is asking for trouble. A large group of tired swimmers going into the water at the tail end of a triathlon is dangerous, too. An exhausted cyclist can slow down and coast. An exhausted runner can walk or stop. But an exhausted swimmer . . . ?

Additionally, in races where swimming is the last event, a large number of the tired competitors end up with leg cramps. Muscles in the calves and hamstrings, worked hard during the bike race and the run, have a tendency to launch themselves into excruciating spasms. You've made a bad situation even worse: it's dangerous *and* painful.

As for the bike/run order, it's more a matter of tradition than anything else. Most people would say that a running finish is more dramatic than a cycling finish. It certainly is more easily controlled from a timing and safety standpoint. If you've ever been to a 10K running race and watched the chutes back up at the finish line, you can imagine what it might be like with bikes.

ARE THE DISTANCES FAIR?

Fair for whom? It is widely acknowledged that swimmers are at some disadvantage, since the aquatic portion of a triathlon usually takes the shortest time. On the other hand, former competitive swimmers make up a disproportionate number of elite triathletes. No one has been able to come up with a good reason for that.

There is an obscure movement within the sport that supports "equidistance triathlons," but the idea has never

5

caught on—largely because these races feature incredibly long swims. The bulk of competitors are simply scared off.

Triathlon distances were never intended to be fair. In the old days in San Diego the distances and the order of events were more whimsical than anything. The Ironman, based on the early San Diego concept, was an arbitrary combination of the three most popular endurance events in Hawaii: the Waikiki Rough Water Swim, the Around-Oahu Bicycle Race, and the Honolulu Marathon. People pushing the

Gruel-a-thons they're not. This is Kirsten Hanssen of Denver, winning the 1986 Bud Light USTS National Championship.

fairness angle raise objections periodically, but the protests are largely ignored; as the sport matures and athletes enter triathlons as "triathletes" rather than as transplanted competitors from other sports, the debate's significance fades.

GRUEL-A-THONS THEY'RE NOT

Contrary to a widely held misconception, most triathlons are not extended sojourns into human misery. They come in several sizes and levels of difficulty, some doable in less than two hours by even the beginner. In fact, relatively few triathletes compete in long races that take hours and hours to complete. Sanity has the firm upper hand.

Here are the official distance designations according to the Triathlon Federation/USA, the national governing body of the sport in the United States:

Short
1-Kilometer swim (.62 miles) or less
25K bike (15.3 miles) or less
5K run (3.1 miles) or less

Short-distance triathlons (you'll often hear them called "sprint" triathlons) are usually low-key and the emphasis is on fun, although there are sprints for the top competitors. This is the distance at which first-timers get their feet wet—literally.

In short-distance triathlons the order of events is often rearranged, and the swim is as likely to be held in a pool as in open water.

One popular short-distance triathlon is Rizzie's Wildman Triathlon, which is held in St. Petersburg, Florida, each spring. The distances are .5 miles for the swim (in the ocean), a 15.5-mile bike ride, and a 3.1-mile run. The winning time for the men in 1986 was a nongrueling one hour, three minutes. The first woman crossed the line in 1:11. Middle-of-the-pack times ranged around an hour and a half; it took the last finisher 20 to 25 minutes longer than that. Average swim times were around 20 minutes, average bike times under an hour, average run times a little less than 30 minutes.

International
1K–2K swim (.62–1.2 miles)
25K–50K bike (15.5–31 miles)
5K–10K run (3.1–6.2 miles)

These are by far the most popular triathlon distances in the world. In 1986 the Bud Light U.S. Triathlon Series (USTS), which uses the now-standard 1.5K/40K/10K format exclusively, alone accounted for more than 20,000 competitors in its 13 races.

The USTS pioneered the international distances, introducing them in 1984 after experimenting with two other combinations in 1982 and 1983. Anticipating skepticism of triathlon by the international governing bodies of the three individual sports, Carl Thomas, a USTS founder, set distances that legislators in each could easily relate to: 1,500 meters for the swim, the longest Olympic swimming event; 40 kilometers for the bike, a common international road-racing distance; and 10 kilometers for the run, a classic Olympic track distance. The entire triathlon was designed so that the top competitors would finish the race in about the time it took to complete the longest continuous Olympic event, the marathon. If the sport of triathlon is ever included in the Olympic Games, it is likely to be at the international distance.

At the USTS race in Phoenix, Arizona, in 1986, the winner finished in 1:58. The first woman finished in 2:12. The last finishers (on a tough course) crossed the line in over four hours. Middle-of-the-pack times were 34 minutes for the swim, 1:20 for the bike, and 55 minutes for the hot and hilly run.

Long
2K–5K swim (1.2–2.5 miles)
50K–100K bike (31–62 miles)
10K–30K run (6.2–19 miles)

The most common long-distance triathlons are called

"half-Ironman distance" events: 1.2-mile swim, 56-mile bike ride, 13.1-mile run, although the distances are hardly standard.

Triathlons in the "long" category are not for beginners. They take the best male athletes well over four hours to finish, the best women around five hours, and are seen by even many experienced competitors as something to point an entire season's worth of racing toward. They are true endurance events, requiring a lot of experience and a full range of knowledge about eating during the competition itself.

None of which is to say that an inexperienced triathlete cannot complete a long-distance race. The question is whether the suffering you'll encounter is worth it. I think not.

Ultra
4K swim (2.5 miles) or more
100K bike (62 miles) or more
30K run (19 miles) or more

The most famous ultra of all, of course, is the Ironman World Championship Triathlon in Hawaii, held each October. The Ironman comprises a 2.4-mile swim, a 112-mile bike ride, and a 26.2-mile marathon. If the distances aren't bad enough, the conditions are extreme—the bike and run courses cross a lava desert and are almost totally unshaded. The temperature rises to well over 100° at midday and the humidity is high. Strong winds usually add to the difficulty.

Triathlon novices have completed the Ironman. Not one to my knowledge has had any better than an awful experience. Their stories are almost always hilarious in retrospect, but they all advise that no one follow their example. One man told me an amazing tale of his first Ironman—for which he was grossly undertrained—then actually searched me out a day later to make sure I didn't suggest that what he had done was smart or admirable. I assured him that I wouldn't.

9

Although entry into the race is getting more difficult every year—there are strict qualification standards and a lottery for nonqualifiers—I highly recommend the event, but only as an ultimate goal. It's probably not a good idea even to think about it before you've got two or three seasons of competition under your belt. Even veteran triathletes usually spend no less than six months training specifically for the Ironman.

As of October 1986, the men's course record for the Ironman was owned by Dave Scott: 8:29:37 (swim: 50:53, bike: 4:48:32, run: 2:49:12). The women's course record was

Dave Scott, whose nickname is "The Man," won the Ironman five times between 1980 and 1986. He is certainly one of the greatest endurance athletes of all time.

owned by Paula Newby-Fraser: 9:49:14 (swim: 57:03, bike: 5:32:05, run: 3:20:06).

There were 959 finishers in 1986; 1,039 started. The last finisher crossed the line at 16:55:44 (the course is closed at the 17-hour mark). The 500th-place time was 12:24:42.

The Triathlon Federation/USA also recognizes two youth triathlon distances (junior and senior), biathlons in all categories (just remove the swim), and "stage" triathlons, which are triathlons in which the events are not continuous. The Ultraman Triathlon in Hawaii, held over much of the same route as the Ironman—except that it is three times as long—is a stage triathlon. It takes three days. On the first day competitors swim six miles and ride 75. On the second day they ride 175 miles; on the third day, 52.4.

The Ultraman is getting near a fifth distance category of triathlons that I call "Stupid." That's a provincial view, I admit, since most people thought the Ironman was crazy when it was first held. There are a handful of fools who have even done triple Ironman events, and I'm sure someone is thinking about doing a quadruple Ironman. To me, these are stunts, not races, and take no more than fuzz in the brain and not much creativity. The best athletes have proved they can actually *race* the Ironman, moving along throughout the day at tremendous speeds. Beyond the Ironman distance, however, simple dead-headed survival is about the only requirement. Better to throw a pack on your back and go hike in the woods.

Obviously, there is a triathlon for every taste and level of fitness. I strongly recommend that the beginner start at either the short distance or international distance, and stay there for at least a year, perhaps two or three. In fact, many excellent triathletes stay there forever, dipping into a half-Ironman-distance event perhaps once a year for variety's sake. In this book I will refer to international-distance events almost exclusively, since they are the entry-level triathlon of choice. Ironman is a goal that every triathlete should have—it's a marvelous experience—but as I mentioned, it is not an event for the beginner.

The budding young stars. These are triathletes in the 15–19 age group at the Bud Light USTS National Championship.

NEVER TOO YOUNG, NEVER TOO OLD

Almost all triathlons include age-division awards in their prize structures. Those that offer prize money usually offer it only to triathletes in a defined professional division. They give some other kind of recognition to age-group athletes in either five- or ten-year increments: medals, ribbons, certificates, etc. The USTS, for instance, gives awards in 10 different age categories in both men's and women's divisions: from 15–19 and 20–24 on up to 55–59 and 60 and over. While women in the 60-and-over division are still rare, there are a great number of men in that group who compete regularly and fiercely. The 1986 USTS National Champion in the men's 60-and-over division, Rudi Schuster, of Norfolk, Virginia, completed the 32-mile international-distance course on Hilton Head Island, South Carolina, in 2:35:30, beating the man in second place by a mere four seconds.

There is even a triathlon series for younger athletes, called Ironkids, with separate distances for juniors (7–8 years; 9–10 years) and seniors (11–12 years; 13–14 years).

WHAT DOES A TRIATHLON LOOK LIKE?

As I've already mentioned, more people compete in international-distance triathlons than in any other variety. Approximately 55 percent of all triathlons held in the United States are of this distance—for good reason. The 1.5K/40K/10K format is a challenge at all levels, from beginner to expert.

Beginners see an international-distance race as a bona fide triathlon, one they can be proud to finish. The experienced age-group triathletes know their best times at the distance, and they know many of their competitors, too. Age-group competition in triathlons across the nation is fierce.

For professional triathletes, international-distance events are a staple of their season. The pros compete weekly, incorporating the races into their training schedule and relying on what they hope will be a regular flow of prize money to pay the rent.

Using the USTS system as a guide, here's how a large international-distance race might go. A time line is indicated, based on a 7:30 A.M. start and a beginner-ish finishing time of two hours and 56 minutes.

THE DAY BEFORE THE RACE

Registration and number pickup—Most triathlons require an athlete to register in advance. The logistics are much more complicated than in the weekend 5K or 10K running races you might be used to, so you won't find too many triathlons that allow competitors to register on race morning. Some races, the USTS events included, even require registered athletes to check in the day before the race to pick up numbers and other materials that will be needed to compete.

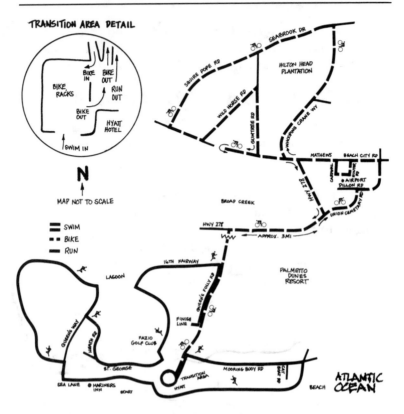

This is what a triathlon course looks like from the air. A map of the course is usually supplied to the competitors in the larger races prior to race day—this particular one is from the Bud Light USTS National Championships in Hilton Head Island in 1986. Most triathletes make every effort to go over the course in a car before the race so that they have an idea of what to expect. It's a good idea; I can't imagine racing without *doing that. Note the transition area detail that indicated the basic traffic flow.*

Prerace meeting—These are common to most large races. Last-minute course changes, special rules, and hazardous areas on the route are outlined. Prerace meetings are usually long and boring, but they're useful, and it's usually the information that you miss that screws up your race. If you're a beginner, you're probably going to be too nervous to do anything else anyway. Going to the prerace meeting is a good idea.

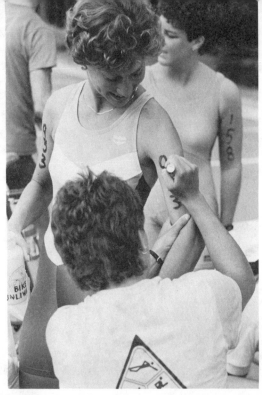

Can't tell the players without a program. Or in the case of triathlons, can't tell them without a number. I've known first-timers to make a point of not scrubbing the things off for a day or two, just to show it off. Why not?

RACE DAY—5:30 A.M.

Race morning check-in—Triathletes are not only identified by paper numbers like runners but by numbers drawn on their legs and arms with waterproof markers on the morning of the race. (The bulk of help in staging a triathlon is volunteer labor. Body-marking ranks at the top of the list of desirable assignments.) Before the swim, bikes are hung in numbered racks set up in what's called the *transition area*. Experienced triathletes arrive early to beat the long lines, then use the extra time to arrange their equipment for the bike ride and the run, warm up, and relax before the start.

In some triathlons, there are two transition areas, one for the swim/bike change, then one for the bike/run change at a different location. A large race with two transition areas is guaranteed to be mildly chaotic at best.

Many large triathlons use wave starts for organizational and safety reasons. The waves are separated by age group, which has the side effect of increasing the intensity of the age-group competition.

7:30 A.M.

The swim—In USTS events, competitors are separated by age groups, identified by different color swim caps, then sent off in waves, with their final times being corrected for the delay by computer. The wave-start innovation was introduced in 1984 in response to the large fields of athletes the USTS was attracting. It is becoming increasingly widespread.

Mass swim starts are perhaps the most frightening part of triathlons for the beginner. In large races without wave starts, timid swimmers learn to start slowly, near the back, a procedure known as self-seeding. The alternative is to be battered mercilessly by faster swimmers coming from behind (and over the top, or however else they can get around).

Triathlon swim courses are usually set in the shape of a

National Champion Kirsten Hanssen getting a light pre-race massage. That's what a tri-suit looks like. She'll swim in it, bike in it, and run in it.

triangle or a rectangle, with the corners marked by bright orange buoys. Or let's say they *should* be marked with bright orange buoys.

Basic rules of the swim: none really, except to stay on the proper side of all the buoys. Most triathletes use the crawl, or freestyle, although beginners in Europe often breast-stroke the entire distance. They look pretty silly, if you ask me. If you're going to be a triathlete, learn to swim. More on that later.

8:01–8:04 A.M.

The swim/bike transition area—Off come the goggles and the cap, on go the cycling shoes and the helmet. Changing tents, which were regular features of transition areas in years past, have all but disappeared in races of less than ultra distances. Triathletes now make few if any changes of clothes during competition. They wear either one-piece lycra-spandex *tri-suits* or simply their nylon or lycra swimsuit through all three events.

17

The Baltimore Bud Light USTS, a large inner-city triathlon that has become very popular.

Marshals on motorcycles are usually assigned to enforce the no-drafting regulations.

8:04-9:25 A.M.

The bike—Triathlons are continuous events, so triathletes start the bike ride as soon as they can get out of the water, get in the saddle, and go. Sometimes they go too hard and fall, either because their legs are still wobbly from the swim, or because they didn't look where they were going. Be careful.

Transition areas are great places from which to watch a triathlon. Not only can you see the competitors close up, but the action is fast and sometimes chaotic—exciting!

Safety is the obvious consideration on the bike, especially for the beginner who may not be confident in a crowd, so stay out of them.

Basic rules: Hard-shell helmets are required. Even if they weren't, you'd be a fool not to wear one. *Drafting*, gaining an aerodynamic advantage by riding close to another cyclist, is strictly forbidden. Tri-Fed requires triathletes to be not less than two bike lengths behind or six feet to either side of each other, except when one is in the act of passing.

Aid stations—Aid stations, staffed by volunteers who dispense water and some kind of electrolyte replacement drink (Exceed, ERG, Gatorade, etc.), should be available at triathlons of all distances. The USTS puts at least two stations on every bike course (and expects athletes to carry at least one full water bottle when they start), and one per mile on the run course. Perhaps no feature of a triathlon is more important to the well-being of the competitors than properly staffed, properly stocked aid stations.

The aid stations at the Ironman are legendary—some of them are several hundred yards long, supplied with everything from water and defizzed Coca-Cola to bananas, oranges, chocolate chip cookies, and jelly sandwiches. An Ironman competitor I know, feeling terrible during the run one year, tried to perk himself up by joking with the volunteers. "What, no quiche?!" he asked as he stumbled through. Everyone laughed, but no one would have been surprised if there had been some warm quiche available. Almost everything else was.

19

Kirsten Hanssen concentrates coming into the transition area on her bike. In most races you'll encounter some system—bumps, cones, etc.—designed to slow you down.

9:25-9:28 A.M.

Bike/run transition area—Transition areas are always exciting. This one is the crazier of the two, and also the more dangerous. Usually the bike/run transition involves a change of shoes only. As you ride into the transition areas of most large triathlons, you will encounter some system designed to slow you down, both for safety and for timing purposes. Traffic cones or speed bumps are commonly used.

Etiquette is important here. Bikes should be racked so as not to interfere with other cyclists; gear should not be left where another competitor is going to run into it.

Basic rules: failure to rack your bike is considered unsportsmanlike conduct and can lead to disqualification.

9:28-10:24 A.M.

The run—The last stage. Usually by this time the morning has heated up, so you should be sure to hit every aid station. If you can't run or walk and drink at the same time,

Four-time Bud Light USTS National Champion Scott Molina heads off into the run. Molina sits while he's changing from bike shoes to running, a better method, I think, than standing, although some of the top triathletes do it that way as well. Note Molina's very basic equipment: just the shoes, his singlet (in his hand), a swim suit, and his sunglasses. If he didn't have to keep his sponsor happy, he'd probably just run in his suit, with his race number around his waist on an elastic strip.

Taking aid along the way is critical in a race. Don't pass up a single aid station. You need to drink before you feel the need to.

The post-race camaraderie is one of the best parts of the day. Feels good to be finished, with a great workout under your belt and good friends on all sides.

then stop and drink. Proper hydration, which will be explained in more depth later, is critical.

The USTS has begun to mark the calves of runners with an age-group code so that athletes can tell if a person in front of them is in the same age group. It tends to liven up the age-group competition a bit—not that it *needs* to be livened, but it's a nice touch that takes some of the guess-work out of the race for age-group awards. You may see the system at other triathlons, too.

The finish line—Postrace camaraderie is a big part of any triathlon. At most races a wide variety of beverages and snack food is available—granola bars, yogurt, and fresh fruit are staples. Massage services are also normally avail-able at the larger races. If you're a beginner, the best part about the finish line is obvious: you've become a triathlete! If you're like most, this is about the time you start thinking about the $2,000 bike you saw last week at the shop. And the new cleats, and the red helmet, and the pink tri-suit with leopard-skin panels, and the . . . good Lord, you've done it now.

SOME GOOD SOURCES OF TRIATHLON INFORMATION

Triathlon Federation/USA
P.O. Box 1963
Davis, CA 95617-1963

Race Series:

Bud Light United States Triathlon Series
P.O. Box 1389
Solana Beach, CA 92075

New England Triathlon Series
430C Salem St.
Medford, MA 02155

Ironkids
200 North Broadway
St. Louis, MO 63102

Publications:

Triathlete magazine
8461 Warner Dr.
Culver City, CA 90232

Triathlon Today!
802 Granger
Ann Arbor, MI 48104

Running & Triathlon News
5111 Santa Fe St., Suite #206
San Diego, CA 92109

One goal of a novice male triathlete, I guess, would be to train so he could look like some of the top guys in the sport. That's two-time Ironman champ Scott Tinley on the right, Ken Glah of Pennsylvania in the middle, and Mac Martin, who placed 10th at the Ironman in 1986.

2
THE CONCEPT OF TOTAL FITNESS

Triathlon is an exciting way to stay fit. A good friend of mine once described it as a "sexy" sport, and I have to agree with him; it's full of high technology and muscles and speed. The clothing is bright and tight, the equipment is flashy, and triathlons themselves are wild and full of action—they tend to sell themselves. The image is terrific.

What good is image? Well, it could be good for a lot. One top triathlete I know—a man with quite an image of his own within the sport—has the insides of the doors to his closet, which is full of workout gear, plastered with action photographs of great performers in running and cycling. Each day before he goes out the door to train, he can psych himself up simply by getting dressed. He can look in the mirror and say to himself, "I'm one of those guys."

Continuing incentive is the key to becoming a triathlete, and the incentive won't always come from training itself. You'll improve quickly in the first months, but you can't expect the rapid improvement to continue indefinitely. (If it does, write to me. I'll be your agent. We'll get rich together.)

Racing in a triathlon is tough, sure, but it has its moments.

You'll have to deal with disappointments and frustrations constantly; it's that way for even the best. That's where image comes in. There will be times when the simple act of lacing up your cycling shoes for an early-morning bike ride will give you a nice, solid rush of being part of something special. It'll be chilly out, and almost everyone you know will still be asleep, and you're heading out to ride 40 miles of hills before breakfast. "Am I crazy?" you'll ask yourself. And you are, a little, but that's part of the package. What you are—even more than crazy—is an *athlete*. And what the heck, the tights look good and the new cycling jersey fits just right. . . .

Commitment is important, but it isn't always easy. Every little bit helps.

From a conditioning standpoint, triathlons keep your entire body strong—lean and mean all over. The swimming and the bike work on the upper body (you'll be surprised how much you use your arms as you improve on the bike);

the bike and the run work on the legs. And because your general level of cardiovascular fitness will be improved and then maintained by all three activities, less time/mileage work will be required in each sport, so the threat of overuse injuries will be greatly reduced.

Besides all that, triathlons are a heck of a lot of fun. They demand a great deal in terms of training and stamina, but the intricacy of moving efficiently from one sport to another in competition is a real kick. Transitions from the swim to the bike to the run are almost events in themselves. Getting "good" at triathlons is not merely a matter of getting fast. Getting "smart" is critical. You can reach performance plateaus in all three sports and still race faster by better organizing your mind and refining your technique.

Strategy is not just for the elite triathlon competitor. If you're a terrible swimmer, chances are you'll gain ground on the bike; if you're a great runner, you can plan your whole race to make up the most ground in the last event. In triathlons, as Yogi Berra said, "It ain't over till it's over."

The level of effort for many of the triathletes in an international-distance race is high—from the start right to the finish.

THE TRAINING EFFECT

Your body reacts to training by becoming more efficient. Your heart grows in size and strength, pumping a greater volume of blood with every squeeze. The number of times it must beat per minute is reduced. The heart of a sedentary person contracts 60 to 70 times a minute; in the body of an aerobically fit individual, it may pump as few as 35 to 45 times a minute, with the total volume of blood increasing slightly.

The exercised muscles get bigger, too, with the muscle fibers expanding and the number of capillaries in the muscle almost doubling in order to handle the increased blood flow.

In addition, the chemical energy factories in the muscles "learn" to be more efficient. Oxygen and fuels are used more readily; waste products are released into the blood stream more directly.

The level of an athlete's cardiovascular efficiency can be gauged by measuring his or her maximum aerobic capacity, or VO_2 max. This is the maximum volume of oxygen (not air) that the athlete can use per minute. Expressed in milliliters of oxygen per kilogram (for the simple reason that large people have a greater total oxygen capacity than small people), a normal, sedentary, 20-year-old man might have a VO_2 max in the 45–50 range. Many trained, elite triathletes have values in the 70s—some even above 80.

VO_2 max values are measured in the laboratory, with the person being tested running on a treadmill or riding a stationary bicycle. While the values are not accurate indicators of endurance potential—some endurance athletes with relatively low maximum values have become champions; high values have not always translated into success—they are helpful in monitoring the effectiveness of a training program, because your VO_2 max will increase as you train.

SPECIFICITY OF TRAINING

"Cross-training" is a term that has been popular in triathlon circles for years. One definition—and the one that is most commonly used—implies that if you are well-conditioned in one sport, your activities in other sports benefit accordingly; that if you trained one leg and not the other, both would end up being in shape.

The idea made a lot of sense. It sure *seemed* logical. But studies by physiologists on trained athletes failed to support the concept of cross-training—at least in the way it was first defined. While there is some carryover in terms of overall cardiac fitness, with the heart becoming more efficient and the muscles of the chest that actually do the breathing also becoming conditioned, the train-one-leg/both-legs-get-fit concept is not accurate.

Training is specific. Being in shape for one sport doesn't mean much when you switch—from marathon running, say, to racquetball. Among the running population of this country are some of the finest cardiovascular machines in history, but they do nothing but run. Off the roads, they're fragile. Wouldn't last more than a minute or two in a weekend touch football game. Or if they did, they'd barely be able to walk on Monday. Their arms would be sore from throwing, the muscles in the backs of their legs and in their butts would ache from all the quick starting and stopping. Put that same runner in the swimming pool and he or she is going to be breathing like a freight train after just a couple of laps.

No matter how efficient your heart is, untrained muscles are not going to work the way trained muscles do. They simply won't have the capacity to handle all the oxygen and fuel that's being thrown in their direction. It's like a city at Christmas time with a terrific mass-transit system and a lousy airport. Getting to the terminal on time, then not being able to fly out, only makes people sore.

Hence the idea of "Total Fitness." In a way, it was the natural successor to the running boom of the seventies, which recognized the need for fitness but defined it in narrow terms. Specialization led to injuries, and perhaps even worse in the long run, boredom. Training in three sports keeps you fitter, and it keeps you better motivated, too. In that sense the term "cross-training" does apply: fitness all over.

As your triathlon training becomes more sophisticated, you'll come to see how the concept of training specificity is applied. You'll experience an initial rush of overall improvement, then a period of stagnation, at which point you'll begin to concentrate on one sport at a time. You'll work especially hard on your cycling for a month, for instance, while leaving your running and swimming at the same levels.

"We all need little victories," 1985 Ironman champ Joanne Ernst once told me. "That's the nice thing about triathlons. You're working in three different sports, so usually things aren't going terrible in all three at once. You've at least got one sport to feel good about all the time."

THE FITNESS LIFESTYLE

There's much more involved in total fitness than just exercising a broad range of muscles. Ideally, your triathlon training regimen should include a constructive nutrition program and allow you to function socially in a world that might not share your views on exercise.

I have a good friend who remembers talking about his training schedule to a journalist during an interview. My friend was espousing his rational, well-balanced theory on how he managed to fit full-time training into his life. "Plenty of time," my friend said. "You've got 24 hours in a day, right? You work eight hours, sleep eight hours, and you've got eight hours to train."

Sounded great. Except that my friend's now ex-wife didn't

People have their own ways of fitting triathlons into their lives.

appreciate the inference—or the reality of his priorities. He had let them get badly out of balance without even realizing it.

If you can make your training work and still keep your job and your spouse, then you're moving in the right direction. On the other hand, if you feel a need to sell out to your partner, file for divorce, and move to San Diego so that you can live near Scott Tinley—all because your swim time for 1.5 kilometers isn't dropping the way you'd like, then you are Totally Lost, not Totally Fit. We're looking for fun and integration here, not fanaticism. If you're going to be unhealthy about being healthy, then you're no better off than the three-pack-a-day smoker who spends five nights a week cuddled up to the bar.

Here's what Tinley said back in 1982 after he won the Ironman: "If I didn't enjoy riding my bike, and I didn't enjoy swimming and running, I would have never entered the race. The point is, you have to enjoy the *journey* leading up to the goal."

Amen.

But you do need to be committed. Incorporating triathlons into your life should be done carefully, but firmly. Unless you're semiretired, with a pool in your backyard and a full gym in your garage, training is never going to be convenient. The best you can hope for is to make it part of your lifestyle. Look for gaps in your daily schedule that can be filled without the loss of something that's important to you. Or make new gaps that you won't end up resenting a month from now. Set up a schedule that takes reality into account. If you don't, you'll experience several months of false starts, then end up discouraged and no further along than when you began—maybe even behind where you started, because now you've failed.

NO PAIN, NO GAIN—WOULD YOU BELIEVE A LITTLE OF BOTH?

The "no pain, no gain" concept is rapidly losing favor within the fitness community. Unlike elite athletes who look only toward achieving goals within a narrow range (the Olympics, a career as a professional athlete, a national championship), recreational triathletes concentrate more on living a lifetime of fitness, even if they compete seriously. The "all-or-nothing" philosophy hardly applies. Whipping yourself unmercifully into shape, launching yourself into each workout like Pete Rose gunning for third, is counterproductive. It'll burn you out long before you've had a chance to find out what this sport really means.

Approach your training with your main goal tucked securely in the back of your mind. Go about achieving it calmly but firmly, with a sense of purpose rather than a sense of urgency. Establish your personal limits by doing slightly less than you think you're capable of, then build from there. Don't go beyond your limits right off the bat, then have to cut back. Retreating is never as satisfying as advancing. Defeats can be motivating, but a steady diet of them is more than anyone can stand.

Caution is one thing, but timidity is another. You must

A hard effort pays dividends in satisfaction and improvement.

test your limits periodically. No matter how "recreational" a triathlete you are or plan to be, improvement in terms of quality or quantity, or improvement at *something*, is the only thing that's going to keep you involved. One reason often cited for the exodus of runners into triathlon is that they became bored with just running. They were looking for new challenges. Heck, you're probably reading this book for the same reason.

In order for improvement to occur, there must be days when training is "hard." You must challenge yourself. There will be days for fast runs and climbing hills on the bike and time trials in the pool. Results don't come without some form of expenditure. I have a feeling that too much emphasis on constant comfort leaves many beginners afraid of reaching for improvement—and deprives them of the tremendously satisfying afterglow of an all-out effort. Competitive athletics do involve some pain. Triathlons do, certainly—no matter what your level of involvement. Knowing when and how to hurt—constructively, not ignoring injuries or going foolishly beyond what you know are your limits—is what proper training is all about.

Mark Allen, one of the premier triathletes in the world. As with all of us, his first workouts after lightening the training load in the off-season take a little extra effort.

EVERYONE NEEDS GOALS

It's unlikely that your first steps as a triathlete are going to be steps of pure joy. The first few weeks are never easy, sometimes not even the first few months. You're going to run into those days when you question the wisdom of your dedication to fitness.

First of all, it's important to understand that you're not alone. Not even the top triathletes in the world jump up and down over the prospect of starting again after a layoff. Mark Allen, five-time winner of the Nice Triathlon in France, found that to be true in 1985 as he geared back up for the coming season. "I think everybody goes through that," he said. "It takes a little while. You start getting tired, and you get an ache here and a pain there. You see someone who has been working out a month more than you have and all of a sudden you think, 'Aww, I shouldn't have taken that time off.' It's hard to work through that. It's where that little bit of self-doubt comes in: 'I'm a year older . . . Am I . . . ?'

"It takes about a month before I start feeling that real strength coming back in."

Allen was 25 years old when he told me that, and a world champion. Plan on giving yourself a little room, OK?

Everyone needs goals. While some people train in three sports for the simple enjoyment of it, most triathletes need to race to feel fulfilled. Certainly, the prospect of competition is a tremendous motivator. Before you start your program, pick a triathlon in your area as an ultimate goal. How far away it is will depend on your level of conditioning. We'll talk more about that later.

Don't depend on that single, long-term goal, however. Set shorter-term goals constantly as you train, and set them relative to your specific ability. If you run a four-mile course near your home for the first time in, say, 40 minutes, an excellent goal would be to run it in 35, but don't try to run the 35 tomorrow. Do it gradually—15, 30 seconds, a minute at a time. Goals are a little like winning at Monopoly; the way up is often a lot more fun than winning.

Goals can keep you locked into a cycle of constant success, providing that you set them intelligently. They are the best motivational tools at your disposal. About the worst thing that you can do is to base your goals on someone else's standards.

THE SEASON NEVER ENDS

After spending years watching top triathletes race, and listening to them talk about how they train and compete, I've arrived at the conclusion that consistency is the most important factor in a successful program.

We are used to seasonal sports—baseball, basketball, on and on. Even triathlons in this country are pretty much seasonal, with most of the events coming between April and October. But the benefits of a year-round program are inestimable. In fact, many professional athletes in the most "seasonal" sports do indeed compete year-round—baseball players in summer leagues in South America, or basketball players in the playground leagues in the big cities.

Not that there shouldn't be periods where the intensity of training changes, or the routine is shifted to a different focus. But a training program that is well integrated into your life should be continued month after month after month. *Lifestyle*—remember? The incredible endurance capacity of triathletes such as Tinley, Allen, Dave Scott, or Scott Molina is the product of a training curve that extends over years, not over just a single season. Their bodies have adapted to competition in three sports in a way that transcends pure talent. Over time, their muscles and bones and body chemistry have come to expect a bike ride after a swim, a run after a bike ride. As the evolution progresses, the efficiency increases tremendously.

I remember Tinley telling me about running a few 6½-minute miles at the beginning of the Ironman marathon in 1982. It was an insane pace. It scared him. "I cut that crap out real quick," he said at the time. He was able to win the race by 20 minutes with a 3:03 marathon—a little over a 7-minute-mile pace. But by 1986 he was running full mara-

Nice race. It always feels good to finish.

thons at the end of Ironman-distance triathlons almost a minute per mile faster. That same year Dave Scott won his fifth Ironman title and posted a 2:49 marathon—better than a 6:30 pace throughout, without anyone close to push him to run even harder.

I'm not suggesting that you have any desire to achieve that level of performance. The point is that getting fit and staying there is perhaps the best way to improve. Raw talent will only get you started.

OVERTRAINING

To nonathletes, the term is absurd. "Overtraining? You mean you go so far as to do too much to yourself? Are you crazy? What kind of an idiot . . . ?"

But it's a big problem. You can get locked into this triathlon thing; locked into the idea that more mileage is better mileage. Despite the fact that you're tired all the time, you think you can solve all of your problems by simply going out for another workout. But what's wrong with that? Isn't working out good for you? If I'm healthy, isn't it good that I try to get even healthier?

No. If you can hit the sack each night enthused about being active in the morning, then you've hooked into a routine that works. If you have to haul yourself out of bed each morning and crawl through another damned five-mile run, then you've gone too far.

Strangely, what many people involved in organized fitness activities forget is that the bottom line is health and maximum performance. All of your fitness-related activities should point toward that, not toward smashing the only body you'll ever have into total exhaustion time and time again. What will that prove?

Overtraining is a danger for even the best, and it's a common affliction of the beginner. The difference is that the beginner is more likely to get injured, or sick—or quit entirely.

I'll talk more specifically about overtraining and some of its symptoms later in the book.

Joanne Ernst, 1985 Ironman champ, and a heck of a short-distance triathlete, too.

3
WORKING TOWARD
THE GOAL

OK, down to business. There are people who've survived even long triathlons without much of a background in any of the three sports, but I wouldn't recommend that. Generally, someone who is poorly prepared for anything but a tiny triathlon is going to have a miserable experience, despite what you may have heard about its being "90 percent mental." Your mind won't take you where your legs refuse to go, believe me.

The same goes for training. You can't do it all in one week. Nor will skills that you've never had or that have been languishing for 20 years magically appear at the mere mention of the word "triathlon." Take it one step at a time.

GOAL? WHAT GOAL?

We're shooting for an international-distance triathlon. That's a 1.5K swim (.9 miles), a 40K bike (25 miles), and a 10K run (6.2 miles). Depending on where you are on the fitness scale, those distances might seem quite modest—or they might seem unapproachable.

They are neither.

Jimmy Riccitello, a top triathlete from Tucson, Arizona, weathers the storm—literally—on a tough day in Boston in 1985.

I don't think you can underestimate the difficulty of any triathlon, no matter what the distance. Race-day conditions, your level of effort, the amount of training you've put in—too little or too much—can make them all tough.

But don't underestimate your own abilities, either. Training, like racing, is simply a matter of putting one foot in front of the other at the start and continuing to do so until you finish. A good and inspirational friend of mine, a guy by the name of Gary Clark, did his first international-distance triathlon six months after his release from the University Medical Center Hospital in Tucson, Arizona. He'd had a heart problem, the biggest kind of heart problem you can have. Not a heart attack, or bypass surgery—Gary had a heart transplant. And he'd been about as unathletic as is possible for 25 years before the operation. He'd been a football player in college, not a runner, or a cyclist, or a swimmer.

Gary did his first triathlon after spending a lot of time trying to convince his doctor that he could do it. As you might guess, he didn't train fast, he just trained steadily. One foot in front of the other. When he crossed the line, he crossed it last, behind everyone, but I'll guarantee that no one who had finished the race—not even the guy who won—felt better than Gary did.

And the moral of that story is to take a look at those distances again and then put your foot out. That'll be a start. Don't stop.

In addition to being doable, international-distance triathlons are the most popular variety, so it's easy to find a race. It's also fairly easy to hook up with several people who have done one—for training advice and occasional encouragement. Also, when the big day arrives, there are likely to be plenty of first-timers.

Gary Clark—he did his first triathlon just five months after his heart transplant operation.

International-distance triathlons are held in a wide variety of locations. If Chicago or Baltimore or San Diego don't do it for you, how about the high desert outside of Phoenix?

Note that when I discuss the three sports individually in Chapters 4, 5, and 6, I'll list both a competitive goal and a training goal. The competitive goal is the length of the segment in an international-distance triathlon. The training goal is a distance beyond the race requirement. Working up to your training goal before a competition will allow you to go into your first race with a measure of confidence—that you can not only go the distance but that you have gone beyond. It's an important point. I've listened to many triathletes waste a lot of physical and mental energy worrying about potential failures. The fewer doubts the better.

Because there are so many variables in training in three sports it's difficult to estimate how long it will take you to get ready. But assuming that you meet the minimum criteria listed below, plan on training for your first international-distance triathlon for six months. You might be able to do it in less time—if you live an active lifestyle right now, you probably will be able to do it in less. Still, take the time. Who knows? You might not only finish the race and enjoy it, you might do well.

For a fairly comprehensive listing of races in your vicinity, pick up a copy of *Triathlete* magazine. It's a monthly, nationally circulated glossy that you should be able to find on a newsstand. I recommend that you sub- scribe; the sport changes quickly, so staying informed is important. Staying motivated is, too. The race reports in the magazine will keep you psyched.

In addition, it's likely that any local running publication will contain a race schedule, and it's likely to be more specific than *Triathlete*. Check your local running store.

Also be aware that many communities have organized triathlon clubs from which you can not only pick up plenty of good information but where you're likely to find a training partner or two. In my experience, triathlon clubs are low-key, casual, and middle-of-the-pack oriented. They're anything but elitist.

INTERMEDIATE GOALS

Your intermediate goals will largely hinge on your individual training program and can include distances that you'd like to achieve, time goals in your training, weight loss, etc. The more defined your intermediate goals are, the more driven you'll be to achieve them and the more satisfied you'll be when you do.

In addition, some intermediate competitive goals along the way to your first big race may ease some of the tension. Triathletes are friendly people—you'll notice that right off—but the races can be intimidating. I'll talk later about using weekend 10K running races as training aids. Make a point to schedule at least one as a goal before your first triathlon. After that, try to schedule in a minitriathlon, a just-for-fun triathlon, so that you can get a feel for the logistics. If none is available in your area, it wouldn't hurt to stage one of your own. Pull a few friends together on a Sunday morning and give it a whirl.

Another great way to get used to the change from cycling to running is to race in a biathlon. To many people, the world of multisport competition looks a lot less fierce without the water to think about. Biathlons are great training tools, and the atmosphere is usually quite casual, so they're a lot of fun. Since they are less dependent on the weather than triathlons, they are staged frequently during the triathlon "off-season."

PRELIMINARIES

Before you start training you should have a basic level of competence in each of the three sports. If you can't stay up on a bicycle without training wheels, if you can't run up a flight of stairs without wheezing and reaching for the phone to dial 911, if you can't get within three feet of a swimming pool without being paralyzed by fear, then you need to rethink the goals we talked about. None of which precludes

One of the best things about triathlon competition is the chance for everyone to succeed. Age-group competition among the men and women is an important part of the action. But even if you haven't got a shot at an award, the races are a heck of a lot of fun.

the possibility of your ever becoming a triathlete, not by a long shot, but you need to take a step back. Your first goals need to be more manageable. Here are the basic levels of skill from which all things beyond will flow:

Swim: *800 yards freestyle (crawl)*
Bike: *15 miles*
Run: *4 miles*

If you can't swim, you need to learn. That's easy to say for someone who knows how, but a different story if you don't. On the advice of a couple of friends who are competent triathletes but who began at zero in the pool, let me offer some encouragement. First, it can be done. "Not only can you do it," said one of my friends, "but you can learn to love it."

He's right.

Second, being afraid of the water is nothing to be ashamed of—you'd be surprised at how many triathletes are scared to death of that first event. The secret to not being afraid is spending as much time in the water as possible in the company of someone you trust. You need to take lessons. You *cannot* learn to swim on your own. OK, some have—and quite well, too. . . .

But *you* can't.

Take lessons.

The best place to learn to swim is your local YMCA or YWCA, or Boys or Girls Club. In cities where a high school or college has a pool, there are often adult education classes in swimming available to the public. It's interesting to note that many triathletes who have taught themselves to swim, or who have pursued triathlons without having strong backgrounds in the water, end up going back and relearning stroke technique from a professional coach—the lack of certain basic skills has begun to handicap their progress. They spend a great deal of time getting over bad habits, too.

The good news is that even if you are a novice swimmer, you can certainly learn to swim while you continue your

The more you practice running after a bike ride, the better and more natural it will feel.

running and cycling. Once you reach a level of confidence in the water, simply insert the swimming into the program you've already established.

If you are confident of your swimming ability but just haven't been in the pool for years, gradually work up to the basic distance on your own. That first 800 yards will seem like a mountain at first, but you'll be surprised how quickly you'll climb it.

The bike ride is probably the easiest of the three sports to build from a base of almost nothing. It's also the sport in which you'll progress most rapidly during the early stages of training. Anyone can ride a bike. You'll be amazed, however, at how much there is to the sport once you get that minimum base established. It's changed a lot since you were a kid.

The run is the most important of the events in which to have a solid base. If you can't go the four miles now, stick to running until you can. Throw in a social bike ride on weekends, just to get a feel for it. If you're a novice runner *and* a novice swimmer, coordinate your efforts to learn the two sports as your schedule allows—perhaps on alternating days. Set aside your organized triathlon program until you've reached the minimum levels. Plunging in too fast will only make the ultimate goal that much harder to reach.

JUST FOR SAFETY'S SAKE

If you're over age 30—and especially if you've been inactive for a number of years—it's a good idea to have your family doctor give you a once-over before you start training. If your family has a history of heart disease, it's important. Why tempt fate and history at the same time?

On the off-chance that your doctor takes one look at you, draws on his cigarette, then scoffs at the whole idea of triathlons, find an athletic-injury clinic or a sports medicine center in your area and get a referral.

The pretraining test is even more important if you're an ex-jock and you've been sitting around for a while, because you're the most likely type of person to exceed your limits. All that "healthy as a horse" business is nonsense.

Note: Even if you are at no risk at all—and if you can afford it—there are some advantages to having your VO_2 max and your body-fat percentage measured, and your blood tested, both before you start your program and again six months or a year down the road. You'll find the gradual adaptation of your body to training fascinating. Plus, the more you know about the way things work, the more apt you are to remain enthused. How can you not stay fit when you can see in black and white how far you've come?

HOW MUCH IS TOO MUCH?

Pacing is not something that comes naturally to un-trained athletes. How do you know when you're going fast enough to do yourself some good? Or if you're really puffing, how do you know you haven't gone too far?

The easiest way is to check your pulse against your *maximum heart rate.*

To determine your maximum heart rate, subtract your age from the figure 220. Now multiply your maximum rate by 70% and again by 80%. This will give you a range for your *target heart rate.* Your normal workouts should move your heart rate into the target range and keep it there. If you're below the bottom level of the range, you're getting less benefit from your training than you should. Over the top and you're moving too close to your maximum—for a beginner at least. Top athletes push it right up there at times, but not too often. Recovery from peak efforts is slow, and the risk of structural injury increases greatly.

Always take your pulse at your wrist with your middle finger. Count it for 10 seconds, then multiply by six. (There's some evidence which shows that taking your pulse beneath your chin, at the carotid artery, triggers your body into slowing the pulse. Counting for an entire 60 seconds gives you too much time to recover.)

Here's what the maximum heart rate and the target heart rate range would be for a 40-year-old man:

$$
\begin{array}{l}
220 \\
\underline{-\,40} \\
180 \text{ maximum heart rate} \\
\times\,70\% = 126 \\
\times\,80\% = 144
\end{array}
\Big\} \text{ target range}
$$

This is a good guide for the untrained individual. If you're in good shape, your sense of pace and your own limits are adequate. Besides, you will recover enough within the 10 seconds it takes to read your pulse to skew the results.

ALWAYS WARM UP
(AND COOL DOWN)

Make it a general practice to loosen your muscles and get your heart working gradually before every training session. Not only will the chance of injury be decreased but you'll end up feeling better during your workout, too.

Warmups are more formalized in swimming than in running and cycling, but the same principle can be applied to all three sports: a warmup consists of the same activity you are *about* to do done slowly. Spend the first mile or so of your run easing into the pace; drift along on your bike for a couple of miles before getting up to speed.

The value of stretching before training is much debated. Some athletes swear by it, some avoid it. Stretching tight muscles is a great way to tear them. I feel that the best answer is to stretch only if you need it. If a calf is tight during the first 400 yards of a five-mile run, slow down and

Warm up before you train and before you race. Stretch lightly, carefully.

stretch that particular muscle gently, without bouncing. If your shoulders are tight during your warmup in the pool, stop and roll your arm around a bit to get things going. Gently, gently, always gently.

After a workout, ease off the pace at which you've been training slowly and gradually. This is especially important if you've been going hard, but it's a good habit to get into in any case. Sudden stops reduce the amount of pumping your heart does, which slows the circulation of blood in your muscles. Waste products that might have been flushed out stay behind. You'll be sore the next day. The common practice of finishing a ride or a run with a sprint to the front door or the driveway is a bad one. It slows your recovery from the workout.

THE TRAINING LOG

You should start recording your daily fitness activities right from the start in a training log, or diary. Some people are better at keeping logs than others, but any log is better than none. If you don't keep one, you'll wish you had somewhere down the line.

Yards in the pool and miles on the road are only two items that should be accounted for. In fact, while they seem the most obvious, they aren't the most important. The point of the training log is not to allow you to brag about the incredible mileage you've been putting in. Rather, it is to identify patterns in your responses to training that are not that obvious at first glance, to fine-tune your fitness program to suit your needs. On what kinds of food does your body perform best? What should you eat before a race? Should you train hard—or at all—on a particular day?

There are no formulas that answer any of these questions. In fact, research on human athletic performance only confirms how differently we all respond to exercise and adapt to competition.

Your emotional response to training is important, too— and it's even more fleeting than what you had for breakfast.

One of the first signs of overtraining is consistent lack of enthusiasm. A good way to track how you feel from day to day is with your log.

One word of caution: you can enslave yourself to your training log. You can lie to it, cheat it, fear it. You can let it force you out the door on days you shouldn't get out of bed.

The training log is a training tool, period. Records of bad days, days filled with lack of self-discipline, are as valuable as days filled with glorious achievement. You're looking for patterns, not pats on the back.

Mileage—Keep track of how much you've done in each sport each day. Make notes about terrain and weather conditions and how you felt about them. Many triathletes name the courses that they cycle or run on a regular basis— "The Drug Store Loop," for instance, or "The Canyon Run." Develop a personal shorthand in your log so that recording the information won't become too tedious.

You're likely to come across the opinion that it's better to run for time rather than distance—30 minutes, for instance, instead of four miles. That way you're better able to run according to how you feel rather than be locked into needing to get from here to there. I don't agree. Every time I've run for time—20 minutes out, say, and 20 minutes back—I've ended up looking at my watch about 300 times. I'm distracted and overanxious, like a 12-year-old waiting for the recess bell. Athletes like goals. Run for goals during your training—to the top of the hill or the Ford dealer near the freeway; you're going to have to do that kind of thing when you race anyway. Just be smart enough to respond to a terrible day by turning around early. If you're feeling too pressured, leave your watch at home.

Diet—According to Dr. Doug Hiller, a Memphis, Tennessee-based physician who has done extensive research on triathletes before, during, and after competition, there is a wide swing on what triathletes burn when they are exercising—from primarily fat to primarily carbohydrate. The best advice, suggests Hiller, is for athletes to eat what works best for them.

Food. Triathletes are known for their appetites. Heck, being able to eat all they want is a reason why many of them compete in the first place.

Diet is a sticky subject, as the flood of fad diets over the years suggests. I remember the uproar at the October 1982 Ironman when Nathan Pritikin enlisted several top triathletes for practical testing of his low-fat theories. Certain medical doctors warned that some of the triathletes might suffer cardiac arrhythmias due to low fatty-acid levels in the blood. None of them did, but the issue of fat in an endurance athlete's diet is still controversial.

To complicate the issue, some people have sensitivities to foods such as dairy products, wheat, or corn. Runners are also known to be prone to diarrhea—either directly because of certain food sensitivities or because of decreased blood supply to the intestine during prolonged, vigorous exercise. All these place restrictions on what an individual can eat with impunity and what not. Recording your basic diet over a period of months can reveal a pattern of success and/

or failure that can be helpful. Dietary philosophy is certainly a matter of individual choice, but if something works time after time—hot dogs or ice cream or steamed brown rice—who's going to fight it?

(A friend reminds me that the amount of food you eat during training is likely to be greater than what you could eat when you weren't. Makes sense; you're burning many more calories. In fact, I've had endurance athletes tell me straight out that one of the primary reasons they train is so they can eat whatever they want. Be careful with that one. It's true in many cases, but you should eat in response to what your needs are, not the other way around.)

Resting pulse rate—As I mentioned earlier, your heart will grow more efficient as you become better conditioned. It will beat more strongly, less often. You'll be able to watch the less-often part happen as you record your heart rate in your training log over a period of months. But a higher than normal pulse rate in the morning indicates that you are not fully recovered from a previous effort. Take your pulse in the morning, before you get out of bed. If it is 10 percent or more higher than is normal for you, take an easy day of training, or take the day off completely. Your body is sending you signals that you shouldn't ignore.

Weight—Here's another tricky subject. There is such a thing as too light. In the past, the running ideal was gaunt, but it was not the look of total fitness.

The best gauge of your weight is your percentage of body fat. A healthy level for men is 10-15 percent; for women 15-20 percent, although many endurance athletes have much lower levels. If you decide to go and have your body fat measured (there are several methods—the water displacement method is the most accurate and most expensive), get an estimate at the same time of what you should weigh. Proceed with that figure (no pun intended) in mind.

If you are training with weight loss as one goal, keep in mind that muscle weighs more than fat. You might even gain some weight at first. That's because your long-dormant muscles are growing in size; your body has begun turning slop into bricks. Be patient, keep working. The results will come. An unexplained, unplanned weight loss of a couple of pounds or more might mean the same thing a rising pulse rate does: that your body needs to rest. If the loss of weight is combined with a drop in your motivation level, then take it easy for a couple of days. You're probably a little overtrained.

Injuries—Record the aches and pains. If you eventually seek treatment for an injury, one of the first things the doctor will ask is, "How long has it been bothering you?" Another: "What makes it hurt?"

Training injuries are difficult to deal with. Some you can train through, some you can't. Having a record of what hurts and when is valuable.

Mental attitude—Had a great bike ride? Had a lousy swim? Feel great about life? Put it all in your log. A consistent lack of motivation can mean that you are training too hard. Or that your schedule isn't working—that you need to sit down and move the pieces around. In time you may discover that there are certain ways of training that make you feel better psychologically. And if you feel better, you'll train better.

Time trials—You should gauge your progress periodically by doing time trials in all three sports: a 1,000-yard swim in the pool, for instance; a 5-to-10-mile bike ride; or a 3-to-5-mile run. The times should be carefully recorded in your log. Schedule them on a regular basis and pencil in blank spaces in advance so you won't forget. You'll be able to match good or poor performances with some of the other categories, such as diet or previous mileage.

Below are a couple of pages from the training log of Joanne Ernst, the women's Ironman Triathlon winner in 1985. They are, in fact, her last two big workouts before the 1986 Ironman. I'm not suggesting that you try to follow her program (please, don't try!), but her log will give you an idea of how a top triathlete keeps track of her progress.

9.30.86 :
Tuesday

∘ a.m. track workout ⌐10 miles⌐
  - 2 mile warm-up
  - 7x1 mile @ 5:46, 5:37, 5:48, 5:46,
                5:46, 5:47, 5:45
      with ~2 minutes rest between repeats
  (a little extra after #3 for blisters)
  - 1 mile warm-down

  Notes : Blisters! Bloody feet! Ouch! Must
      wear socks with Sock Racers at IRONMAN;
      Felt Strong . Great!

∘ noon swim : ⌐3500 yds.⌐
  - untimed : 1100 yds.
  - 4x50 on :50 @ ~:35
  - 3x300 on 4:00 @ 3:46, 3:47, 3:50
  - 3x300 on 4:30 @ 3:47, 3:48, 3:48
  - 1x400 @ 5:07
      Good swim for being dead tired. Had a
  really hard time of it today.

  Notes : 1. Terrible blisters from Sock Racers — has me
      concerned about what I should wear at IRONMAN...

The notes are fun to read through—for the beginner and old hand alike. Much of what Joanne recorded will become more clear after I get into specifics in the next chapter. For now, I think her emphasis on the emotional aspect of training will probably strike a chord.

Note the careful attention to warming up (w.u.) before

10·1·86:
Wednesday

Did my last long day today – hooray!

o Rode [100 miles] @ 5:05:51 : loop / Beach loop /
2× Cañada. Average 19.7 mph – <u>very</u>
good considering the hills and that it was
<u>WINDY</u> on Cañada. The reporter from <u>USA Today</u>
went with Jim to be aid station in
San Gregorio and on Cañada (Jim was
able to show him a lot). Felt pretty good
though my legs are tired from yesterday and
especially noticeable when out of the saddle.
     – Drank: 5½ bottles Exceed
      – Ate: 1⅔ banana (dropped ⅓)
             3 granola bars
     – Also: 1 Excedrin @ ~83 miles (helped!)
Excellent effort! Best of this loop all season!

o Ran [~3 miles) after the ride. Jim rode along
with me – said I ran ~6:30/mile pace. Great!

<u>Notes</u>: 1. Blisters & black toenails a continuing problem.
      Socks do seem to help.
    2. Hamstring butt on right side sore today from
      yesterday. Should be ok in a day or two.
    3. So glad to have the hard work behind me.
    4. Drank 1 glass of high carbohydrate after
      workouts. Ate pancakes/hash browns for lunch.
      Good carbos!
    5. Experimenting with the REVOS – I like them
      though they get streaky from sweat.

the track workout on 9/30/86, and the warmdown (w.d.—
which I referred to earlier as the cooldown).

The record of what Ernst ate during her long ride on 10/1
is interesting. Logistics are of great importance to a triathlete. Ernst's are especially so, since she was putting the final
edges on her Ironman preparation. And it goes beyond

food. The fifth entry under "Notes" refers to a new piece of equipment (and a new sponsor), Revo Sunglasses.

Endurance sports are interesting in that they blur the distinction between the sexes in terms of potential and ultimate achievement. Only a small percentage of competitive triathletes are able to stay with the top women, even in short triathlons. At the Ironman, the top women are always well within the top 50 contestants to finish—out of 1,000. Ernst's diary makes this point clearly. Her ability to run an intense 10-mile track workout one day, swim 3,500 yards, then ride a hard 100 miles the next is the result of years of training. These two pages represent the highest levels in the sport for a man or woman—a level that few ever need to achieve. But they sure give you something to shoot for.

SOME TRAINING SUGGESTIONS

Make sure you're well hydrated—Chronic dehydration is not uncommon among triathletes. There are a number of physiological problems that can result, including electrolyte imbalances that can greatly affect your performance. Drink more than you think you need and always drink after a workout. Keep in mind that you lose a lot of fluid when you swim—you're just not always aware of it. Dark yellow

When it gets hot, stay wet!

This was the Detroit Bud Light USTS event in 1986. It was hot and humid. Most of the triathletes wore nothing but the bare minimum.

urine is one sign that you are low on water. Triathletes and marathoners use this general guideline for proper hydration before a long race: "Drink until your urine runs clear."

Endurance athletes trying to achieve maximum leanness will sometimes dehydrate themselves on purpose. This is not only dumb but it's counterproductive. When you are seriously dehydrated, fluid will pool in your extremities because of poor circulation. You'll end up looking like the Sta-Puf Marshmallow Man.

Make your long workouts fun—If you're off on your first 50-mile bike ride or 10-mile run, you can make things a lot easier for yourself by having a friend meet you at a prearranged destination. It's easier to run from here to there than from here to there and back again. Meet for breakfast or lunch or something. Make an occasion of it. Some of my best long runs have been on holidays. I've run to my sister's house on Thanksgiving and had my mom and dad meet me with some clothes.

Train in terrible weather—You can avoid training on days when it's raining or blowing hard, but it's sometimes more fun to go out anyway. I'm from the John Madden school of triathlon: the more mud and grit and crud you can get through, the better. A Christmas run in the snow is about as good as it gets.

Learn to use the elements to your advantage. I've seen the threat of rain on the morning of a triathlon shake up even some of the best, but I've also seen the look in the eyes of others that said, "Good, it's gonna be tough." Marc Surprenant, a top triathlete from the Cape Cod area, is always at his best when the conditions are bad. Not only does the rain not bother him, it gives him a psychological advantage over most of his competitors.

"When conditions get nasty I go inside myself more," said Surprenant. "I tend to focus better, which lets me race closer to my potential. I'm at my best in situations where other people let the conditions bother them—where they're at their worst."

Use videotape whenever you can—What you are feeling is not always what you are doing. It usually isn't. If you have access to a video camera and to someone who can use it, grab both (the camera and the cameraman), head out on the bike or the run or to the pool, and "Roll tape!" Be a star. There is no better teaching technique available.

You can add to the tape's usefulness by watching the replay with a friend or training partner. Review the points you'd like either to fortify or change, then have the friend watch you during subsequent workouts. In effect, you'll be training your own private coach. The best situation of all is for you to return the favor and coach your coach.

Marc Surprenant is one of my favorite triathletes. He's a gutsy competitor who loves to race when the conditions make everyone else wince.

The start of the Chicago Bud Light USTS race in 1985.

4
THE SWIM

The competitive goal: 1-mile water swim
The training goal: continuous 1.5-mile swim
Basic equipment: nylon or lycra-spandex competitive
swimsuit ($15–$40), a pair of
swimming goggles ($6–$25), regular
access to a swimming pool (20-yard
minimum—$250,000 to $1.2 million
in case you'd like to have your own)

First, you'll need somewhere to train. Despite the fact that
your competitive swimming as a triathlete will take place
in open water, most of your training will happen in a pool.
Two reasons: One, the obvious problems with climate. Not
many of us are fortunate enough to live near a large body of
water that is warm year-round. Two, current training
methods require the controlled environment of a pool. The
road to success in swimming is paved with 25-yard
increments.

Now, how to train? If you're a confident swimmer with

61

perhaps a touch of competitive background in the sport, the best thing you can do is join an organized team or club, then train under the supervision of a coach. You'll get much better much faster. The coaching helps a great deal, and so does the peer pressure. Proper technique in the water is important. Aquadynamics has a lot to do with how hard you have to work to get through that mile in competition—and how much you have at the end to take into your bike ride and your run. That's what a swim coach is for. And swimming in a lane with four or five people who are close to you in ability, supportive of your efforts but also slightly competitive, will push you consistently beyond levels that you can achieve on your own.

There is a well-established national Masters swimming program, with teams or clubs in many cities. While Masters swimming was founded with the competitive swimmer over 20 years old in mind, many triathletes have found places in Masters groups all over the country. The nice part about Masters swimming is that the participants range in age from 20 to 90 with a corresponding range in ability levels. If you do decide to join a team, talk to the coach about your goals. Make him or her aware of your needs: that you are training for triathlons and need a program that will focus on developing your ability as a distance freestyler.

There are several drawbacks to joining a Masters program, however. First of all, they tend to be quite intense. As I mentioned, most of the people in the group will be swimmers—first, last, and always. For the beginner, or for the recreational triathlete who wants to keep the intensity level down, a competitive Masters program can be intimidating. It's also quite possible that you'll run into a coach who gives little credence to the sport of triathlon, or one who will not be much help in smoothing out problems with your stroke. I know, I know, that's what coaches are for. But as with anything else, there are good ones and bad ones.

I myself was fortunate in two regards: I'd been a competitive swimmer as a kid, and when I got back into the pool to train for triathlons, it was with a coach who was willing

This is my favorite shot of Scott Molina. They call him "The Terminator," and he plays it up for fun once in a while. The only time he takes himself seriously is during the race; then he takes himself very, very seriously. The guy is tough.

to . . . no, *enjoyed* accommodating all levels and ambitions in his program. He had some national Masters champions and record-holders in the middle lanes, some honest-to-God beginners in the far lane, and then a group of distance swimmers over on the left—triathletes among them—who provided a bit of comic relief. I'll never forget those first couple of workouts—for which I was entirely unprepared—having to sit on the steps and catch my breath while everyone else in my lane swam on. Embarrassed? I could have been, but the coach thought enough to come over every so often and ask if I was doing OK, and to reassure me that I was not, in fact, going to die. It was a thoughtful, intelligent way to work, and I've been recommending his program ever since. If you ever get to San Diego and need a place to swim, look him up. His name is Ron Marcikic—they call him "Sickie"—and the last I heard, he was running the program at the University of California/San Diego.

Unfortunately, not everyone is so lucky to have a program like that available. Before you do anything, I'd recommend you become confident on your own: swim laps, get strong. Only then should you consider becoming more serious. Find out where the local Masters group trains and simply watch a couple of workouts. Go so far as to talk to the man or woman in charge and see if they'd be comfortable with you—and vice versa. If it looks good, go for it. It really will help.

If it doesn't work, or nothing is available, or you're simply not willing to spend the money (a not uncommon restriction, believe me), it's not the end of the world. As I've already mentioned, many triathletes do train quite successfully on their own. But don't just jump in day after day and swim lap after lap. On a steady diet of long swims you'll reach a performance plateau quickly and then go nowhere. You'll find that working out with one or two friends will be a big help.

BASIC TECHNIQUE

Before you even think about being "correct," you have to be relaxed in the water. Build to that comfortable 800-yard continuous swim we talked about in Chapter 3. If you're constantly struggling to get to the end of the pool, your mind will be on survival and not improvement. Once you're able to go the minimum distance, here are the critical points to consider, along with some suggestions as to how to make them work:

Body position—It should be horizontal, with as little side to side movement as possible. Think of a taut wire, attached to both ends of the pool and running from just above the

This shot shows the high-elbow, thumb-down hand entry position. Note the lead swimmer with his head up, making sure that he's moving in the right direction.

center of your forehead through the middle of your body. All of your movements—stroking and breathing—take place along this axis. A common error is fishtailing from side to side as the arms swing out of the water to stroke or the head pulls up to breathe. Since forward movement is the objective, it stands to reason that lateral movements of any kind should be avoided.

Kick—Use it for stability only, to keep your legs in the horizontal position. You don't want to waste energy by kicking—you'll need your legs later during the bike and run. Kick lightly from the hips, with only the slightest flex in the knee. Try to keep your feet slightly pointed and pigeon-toed.

Arm stroke—Your hand enters the water in a slicing movement, fingers first, about half an arm's length in front of you. Keep your elbow high, and place your hand in the water just to the outside of that central axis. If you reach to the center, or across it, you'll weave through the water like a snake.

Extend your arm underwater, and let the momentum of

65

the thrust continue for a moment as your hand sinks below the surface. How long is a moment? Wait until all the little bubbles disappear. Then begin to pull the palm of your hand down and out, away from the center line, gradually bending your arm at the elbow. The outward pull establishes the momentum of your underwater stroke. Once you've gotten a good handful of water (your hand has traveled maybe eight inches), pull your hand back toward the center line. When your hand reaches about the middle of your chest the pull becomes a push. Press back and toward your outside leg, finishing the stroke with your thumb nearly brushing the outside of your midthigh. The entire stroke, viewed from below, takes an S-shape: pull down and out, pull toward the center, push away.

It's important to keep your wrist tight, hand firm, and fingers loosely together. If you're doing it correctly, the muscle between your thumb and the back of your hand will get tired and sore. Many beginning swimmers get the pull part of the stroke all right, but then let their wrists and hands get floppy during the push. You'll notice that as you get tired, it will be harder to finish your stroke; the last part of the push phase will tend to get sloppy.

As you pull your arm above the surface of the water, concentrate on lifting with your elbow and merely swinging your hand easily beneath it. Sickie has his swimmers practice this movement by having their thumbs actually trace a wake through the water as their arms come across the surface. The key word during the recovery is "relax."

You might also keep in mind that in rough water you'll want to bring your hand higher than in a pool, so it won't get snagged in the chop. The elbow still stays high, though.

Breathing—Breathe by turning your head to the side as your arm finishes toward the end of the stroke, just before your arm comes out of the water. There's a little trough created by the path of your head through the water. Turn (you don't need to lift at all) as little as possible, and turn *only* your head—as if someone were using it as a doorknob. The more you turn your head and the more of your body

66

that goes with it, the greater the chance your alignment will be skewed. A good hint is to wait until you see your opposite arm enter the water before you turn to breathe. Another would be to follow your breathing-side arm with your head as your arm travels through the stroke.

Make sure you exhale underwater before you turn to take a breath. Exhale forcefully so that the intake of air when you turn will be quick and natural.

Many swimmers breathe with equal comfort to either side. It tends to balance their stroke and lets them better gauge their competition during races. The technique—called bilateral breathing—feels awkward at first, but it's a great navigational aid for triathletes. On mornings when the sun is shining right into your eyes on one side, you've got an option.

Some people are more buoyant than others. Runners converting to triathlons often have a hard time becoming confident swimmers because they are lean and lack buoyancy. If this is a problem, you might work on your stroking and breathing techniques while swimming with a *pull buoy*. The pull buoy is made of two cylindrical foam floats connected by cord or a strap. Swimming pools that sponsor competitive teams usually have them locked in a cabinet somewhere. Ask the lifeguard. Or you can buy one. Most large sporting goods stores that carry competitive swimsuits stock them.

Squeeze the pull buoy between your legs, just above the knee or higher—wherever it's comfortable. This keeps you from kicking and therefore isolates your arms; it also keeps your legs floating high so that you can concentrate on stroking, not drowning. Don't get too attached to your pull buoy, however. You can't use them in triathlons.

INTERVAL TRAINING—LIFE IN THE FAST LANE

The intensity level of training in swimming is much higher for longer periods of time than in cycling or running. The reason is simple: since swimming is a nonimpact sport, the chance of injury is relatively small. (Although if you're stuck with lap swimming during busy hours at a public pool, you may disagree.)

Contemporary training methods in swimming make interval training a staple. If you're planning on swimming with an organized group, expect almost all of your yardage, except for warmups, cooldowns, and time trials, to be in the form of intervals.

This is perhaps the greatest argument for going out and finding a team and a coach—or at least a training partner or two. It's next to impossible to push yourself effectively and consistently through an interval program.

Interval training pits a strictly defined workload against an athlete's ability to recover within a specific period of time. If the interval is too ambitious, the athlete is defeated; the workout degenerates into continuous (and usually demoralized) lap swimming. If the interval is too generous, the purpose is defeated; the time requirement is easily achieved, and the rest period is too long.

Intervals are done in "sets." For instance, a 1,000-yard portion of a workout may be in the form of ten 100-yard swims, each swim performed within a two-minute interval—you have that period of time in which to swim 100 yards *and* rest. You push off the wall and launch into the next 100 every two minutes. The entire set takes 20 minutes. On paper it would be noted like this: 10 × 100 @ 2 min.

There are other kinds of intervals, too. Some offer a specified period of rest, regardless of how fast the swim is; some are more complicated constructions—"ladders" of increasing and/or decreasing distances. If you do get involved with a team, the coach's job is to explain all the variations and set the appropriate intervals. If you're on your own, stick with the first example.

There are several sample swim workouts in Chapter 7, along with specific guidelines on how to establish the correct interval for a particular distance.

Long swims are for building your mileage base and confidence. In a pool, they get a bit tedious, especially if you've been existing on a steady diet of intervals. Learn to live with that tedium—you may find that the .9-mile swim in your first triathlon will drag, too. Once you're well into your program, use a timed 1,000-yard swim every other week to check your progress. Experiment with various focusing techniques that make the extended period in the water not only bearable but perhaps even enjoyable.

(There are so many individual variables to proper stroke technique, so much to learn about your own movement and efficiency, that boredom is a problem only if you convince yourself that you're bored. Every swim is different than the one before. Sure, there are going to be bad days when you just can't get through the water, but you probably shouldn't be in the pool on those days anyway. Strive to find the particular rhythm on any one day that gets you into that can-go-forever feeling.)

SOME POOL TRAINING SUGGESTIONS

Your swimsuit will last a lot longer if you make a habit of rinsing it in fresh water after each workout.

Your hair will last longer if you wear a cap when you swim and use a chlorine-neutralizing shampoo afterward.

Your marriage will last longer if you throw your wet towels in the dryer as soon as you get home. Leaving them in your bag for three days is gross.

Take care of your ears. "Swimmer's ear," an infection of the ear common among swimmers (obviously), spring-board divers, and water polo players, is painful. There are several commercial preparations on the market that will help dry out your ears and keep them infection-free as well.

If you don't have one already, buy a water-resistant wrist chronometer, with stopwatch and countdown modes. If you're not swimming with a team and there is no pace clock at poolside, trying to keep track of things using the regular clock on the wall will drive you crazy.

Etiquette: Lap swimming is usually done in circles, moving counterclockwise. Hug the right side of the lane and pass a slower swimmer only at the turns. Assess your ability level accurately and move to another lane if you're wrong. Being much too fast in a lane is as bad as being much too slow.

Don't be intimidated by all the flip turns the first time you walk into a pool—even if the people doing them are your new training partners. In the first place, a flip turn looks fancy but it's easy to learn. In the second, who needs it? You're looking to get fast in open water, not in the pool. Relax, would ya?

OPEN-WATER TRAINING

Of all the obstacles beginning triathletes face, the toughest hurdle is often the swim—not because of the distance but because of the environment: no lane lines, no walls to hang onto, lots of bodies moving in the same direction at the same time. And, of course, there's always the fear of strange beasties. If you're apprehensive about the idea of a long, open-water swim, you are by no means alone.

Practice. Even if you have to drive some distance to do it, practice. It's the only way. And the best way to practice— and to help overcome a fear of open water—is to find a group of Masters swimmers or triathletes and go together. Make an occasion out of it. Old Sickie used to get his Masters group together every Friday night at the La Jolla Cove near San Diego for an ocean swim. Husbands and wives would bring along wives and husbands, singles would bring along themselves plus a friend, and everyone would bring along a hibachi and something to eat. The swimmers would go off in casual groups according to ability, and then everyone would sit on the grass and have dinner. Great fun.

Swimming alone in open water is never a good idea. There's not enough margin for error. And while the likelihood is small that something nearby is going to eat you, lonely brains can tell their owners some strange stories. No sense in scaring yourself to death.

(A semihysterical friend reminds me about sharks. No, he actually wrote it this way: "What about SHARKS?!?" I don't know about sharks, actually, except that I'm not aware of any triathletes ever having been attacked, and that a shark attack even in Southern California is so rare that it makes headlines. As I said, don't swim alone. Take common-sense precautions about swimming in unfamiliar water even with a group. When you look at the statistics, you'll see that riding your bike is a heck of a lot more dangerous than swimming in open water.)

Navigation is obviously important. If you don't look where you're going, a small error at the beginning of a swim can put you a long way off the mark a half-mile out. Sight a landmark, if possible, before you start: the opposite shore, or an anchored boat. You'll quickly learn that things don't look the same when you're swimming as when you're standing on the shore, so you'll have to compensate.

During the swim, raise your head every 10 strokes or so to confirm your position. If you've got a consistent tendency to pull to the right or left, work on correcting that temporarily during the swim itself—sight more frequently—then try to correct it permanently in the pool by swimming with your eyes closed. Whack! Nothing cures you of misdirected swimming better than smacking your head into a tile wall a few times.

There are several methods for sighting as you swim. You can look after you take a breath by swinging your head forward, or look as your opposite hand comes out of the water. Whatever method you use, it will be tiring. Practice in the pool, and occasionally swim a few laps with your head held up and forward to get in shape.

The last resort during a swim is to simply stop and take a good look—you won't lose that much time, and it's a heck of a lot faster than getting lost.

In addition, practice sighting on the people swimming next to you, using them as a guide. (Another point in favor of bilateral breathing.) Don't follow them blindly, of course—they may be worse at navigating than you are—but not having to look ahead frequently will save a lot of energy.

Sometimes getting in the water is the toughest part of the whole day.

Poor vision can be a problem. Quite a number of triathletes wear their contact lenses in the pool during training and throughout races (with goggles over their eyes, of course). If you're wary of that solution, there are prescription inserts for goggles on the market now that I've heard work well. By all means do *something*; not being able to find your way to the showers after a workout in the pool is one thing, losing your way in open water is something else.

Cold water is a real danger to open-water swimmers. It's the bane of triathletes. Extended immersion in water below 65 degrees can result in hypothermia—a lowering of core body temperature, with the resultant loss of muscle function in the extremities. And not only do your arms and legs get numb, but your mind does, too. That's the real danger: not being able to think clearly enough to know what to do when you need to.

Besides avoiding cold water completely, there are several ways to deal with it:

72

Acclimate yourself gradually. If you anticipate having to compete in cold water, swim for progressively longer periods of time in water that approximates race conditions. Spend 10 minutes the first day, 12 the next, and so on. If you find that you just can't handle it, don't press the point.

Wear protective clothing. The first line of defense is your head, where most of your body heat is lost—up to 60 percent. Wear two latex caps. Even better, buy a neoprene diver's cap—the kind with the strap under the chin—and wear that under the thin latex one.

Wear a wetsuit. Wetsuits are increasingly popular in triathlons, even in races where the water temperature is quite warm. Quite simply, they make you a lot more buoyant, which makes you much faster, especially if your stroke technique causes your legs to drag. The flip side of the coin is that they're tougher to get off in the transition area, so you'll have to make the call.

In general, if you have any doubts about your ability to handle the cold, play it safe and wear a wetsuit. (Current rules do allow a race held in warm water to forbid the use of wetsuits. It's best to check in advance.)

Out of the water after a long swim. Keep your head up, watch where you're going. If you've walked through the routine before the race, you should be able to spot your bike right away.

Practice riding your bike after you swim. Remember the specificity of training that I talked about in Chapter 1. The more pieces of the triathlon that you can string together—even casually—the better. If you can ride your bike to swim practice, do it. At first you'll be amazed at how much swimming takes out of your legs. But riding there and back even once or twice a week will make a big difference.

When to train—The thought of swimming first thing in the morning is terrible, but many Masters groups swim before work, and once you're into the routine it's not a bad way to start the day.

Because swimming is the only one of the three sports in which you are almost entirely dependent on someone else's availability (unless you have your own pool), set your swim schedule up first, then work the bike and the run around it.

COMPETITION

Your first triathlon may start in one of three ways: *running* toward the water from a position higher on the beach; *standing* in the water; or *deep water*, in which the

A running start for the swim is one of several options a triathlon race director has for getting things moving. It's certainly the most dangerous—and is losing favor as a result.

A safer alternative to running swim starts are deep-water starts. Here the professional wave of the Phoenix Bud Light USTS moves down to the starting position.

entire field is treading water when the signal comes.

Of the three, the running start is the most hazardous, and it's losing favor for that reason. The deep water start is perhaps the most intimidating for the less-than-confident. In any case, mass swims are never easy for the inexperienced triathlete. Even if you are a sure, strong swimmer, the crush of bodies racing for that first buoy can scare you. Frightened, you're liable to find yourself breathing hard right from the beginning, unable to recover from the first rush. Here's a list of 10 suggestions you can go over before the start to help keep that from happening:

1. Be calm. Make being calm before the gun goes off your first goal of the day. The swim is only one of three parts of the race; the start of the swim is only the first part of one event. There's plenty of time to make up lost ground.

2. Make sure that your goggles are seated correctly. Last-minute fumbling is only going to make you anxious. Leaking goggles during the swim are a real distraction and will cut down on your ability to navigate.

3. If the water is not too cold, get wet and take a brief warmup. That will chase away some of the butterflies. Keep in mind that you may have to stand around afterward and wait for the start—the butterflies might come back *and* you'll be shivering. Plan accordingly.

4. Trace the course in your mind carefully. If you choose to warm up, look for the first buoy from water level. Check your landmarks.

5. Just before the start take several deep breaths. Concentrate on relaxing.

6. Make sure you're near people who seem to be of your own ability. If you have doubts, err on the side of reason,

A deep-water start. It's cold! The triathletes are more than ready to get moving.

It's a good idea to check out the swim course before you start. Always know where you're supposed to go, and pick landmarks that will help you navigate. Things will look a lot different once you're in the water.

not ego; just before the start, move to the back or to the outside of the group. The process is called "self-seeding," and it would work a lot better than it does if everyone wasn't so worried about saving a few seconds. (A friend tells me he always starts to the outside, that he'd rather swim a little farther than fight the congestion. He feels he ends up with a faster time in the long run.)

7. *Don't sprint at the sound of the gun.* Swim at a steady, comfortable pace. If the crush of swimmers becomes too much, don't be afraid to start breaststroking to catch your breath and your bearings.

8. *Don't get mad.* With people flailing away—and sometimes making contact—on all sides of you, it's easy to get frustrated. That will only waste valuable energy. Keep in mind that you're probably the only smart one of the bunch—by the end of the swim, they're all going to be exhausted, and you're going to be fresh. Most important is to protect your goggles.

Mass swim starts can be hectic, confusing, frightening. The best thing to do is take off at the back, or off to one side, or both. Let everyone else beat their brains out for that first 200 yards.

9. The entire crowd is going to bunch again when you hit the first turning buoy. If you're swimming a rectangular course and the first buoy is close to shore—200 yards or less—stay back until the bulk of the pack goes around. If you're too close inside you're going to get squished. (Although if the field is not too tight for your comfort, the closer to the buoys you get, the better.)

10. Generally, take the first 200 yards or so to warm up. Wait until the field stretches out before you start to go hard. The psychological benefits of passing people during the last half of the swim are tremendous.

Preparing for the bike ride is largely a matter of going over the transition in your mind as you reach the end of the swim. Trace the route mentally from the water's edge to the transition area. You might try breaststroking the final 25 yards or so to get the blood moving in your legs. Don't get so psyched up by the crowd at the finish line that you sprint to your bike and then collapse, out of breath. Take your time. Efficiency at this stage makes a lot more sense than flash.

Coming out of the water in a well-organized triathlon, you shouldn't have any doubt as to which way to go.

OPTIONAL EQUIPMENT

Gadgetry has worked its way into swimming just as it has into cycling and running, although to a lesser extent. After all, the only thing you really need is a swimsuit, and everything else has to be waterproof. Some of what's listed below can be lumped into the category of serious training aids, some into the categories of foolishness or fun, whichever is your choice.

Swim fins—Anything that increases the amount of water you push, thereby increasing the workload, will make you stronger. The term commonly used is *resistance training.* Fins make you go fast, but they're tough. Your legs will burn. They also increase ankle flexibility. Watch for hip or knee pain. Muscle soreness is to be expected, but sharp pains or joint pains should tell you to put the fins away for a while.

Hand paddles or webbed gloves—Like the fins, they provide increased resistance. I prefer the gloves. They're much easier to use. The paddles are good for refining your stroke technique—you simply can't keep them on your hands unless you're pulling and pushing correctly. Watch out for sore shoulders and elbows.

Swimsuits with pockets—These are the latest variation on the resistance theme. The suits have several catch-pockets that cup the water and create drag. I suppose that if you combine a drag suit with hand paddles and a weight belt or two, you could make a 200-yard swim feel like a marathon. But you could drown before you ever got to the end of the first lap, too.

Swim tethers—Here you go. With so much on the market to make you feel as if you're almost standing still no matter how hard you're working, tethered swimming goes all the way: you are! If you've got a small pool in your backyard, buying a tether system is much cheaper than tearing up the yard and expanding. (But talk about boring . . .)

Kick boards—They're used to isolate your legs. Triathletes have less need to kick than any swimmer, and you probably would use kicking either to rest or simply break up a workout. (A friend put it less delicately: "Screw the kicking!" he told me. I'm prone to agree.)

Pull buoys—I already discussed their use. These are of great value to triathletes, but don't become too dependent on them.

Underwater music systems—Several brands of aquatic versions of the Walkman are on the market. You're probably much better off concentrating on going faster.

INJURIES

Happily, they are not a major factor in swimming. Shoulder and upper arm injuries are the most common and are frequently caused by overuse of training aids such as hand paddles. Be careful. If you feel a twinge, swim without them.

All the money and state-of-the-art equipment in the world won't help you go faster if you don't sit on the bike like you mean it. Professional triathlete Ken Glah looks like he does.

5
THE BIKE

The competitive goal: *40 kilometers (24.8 miles)*
The training goal: *40 miles at a moderate pace*
Basic equipment: *10-speed bike with toe clips ($450–$800), pair of cycling shoes with cleats ($50–$80), cycling shorts ($20–$35), hard-shell helmet ($35–$60), stationary trainer ($120–$350)*

A friend of mine who was an accomplished international-level performer in cycling, and who became an accomplished triathlete as well, once told me that the reason so few cyclists have come into the sport of triathlon is because they already have a sport they can enjoy. Swimmers, he said, get bored with all the laps and come into triathlons because it's more exciting. Runners get bored with 10Ks and get tired of being injured all the time. Cyclists, though, can't imagine putting themselves through the agony of running or the mind-numbing training of swimming. And why should they? They're never bored.

A triathlete racks his bike. Note the racks and the numbered spaces. Rules require that you return your bike to the spot that's been assigned to you. Courtesy requires that you keep your equipment in that spot and don't let it interfere with another competitor.

Dave Scott off his seat, climbing.

There's probably a measure of truth in what my friend says. Certainly, the cycling is the most exciting part of the triathlon—the fastest, most dangerous, most complicated part. The chance for noncyclists to get involved to some degree in competitive cycling is probably one good reason for triathlon's tremendous growth in popularity during the 1980s.

The challenging technology of cycling is an attraction, too. Triathletes are notorious for being hungry, cost-is-no-object consumers of cycling equipment and clothing. In fact, the cycling industry was pretty stodgy before the triathlon boom came along and kicked it in the rear end, splashing the scene with flashy colors and revitalizing the mass-market demand for state-of-the-art machinery.

You certainly don't need to roll out the big bucks and jump headfirst into the technology scene to become involved in triathlons, but even from a conservative point of view, a basic level of knowledge is a nice thing to have. Let's start there and work up.

CHOOSING YOUR WEAPON

Many beginning triathletes have enjoyed their first race riding a rusty clunker rescued from a far corner of their parent's garage. I hate being seen as a purist, so I'll say first that if that route is either a financial necessity or your preference, go for it. You will certainly be able to race an international-distance triathlon without a major financial investment. You really only need a bike that will hold together, a pair of sneakers, and a helmet. People have done triathlons on single-speed bikes, three-speeds, beach cruisers, and mountain bikes. People have competed on bikes that were so old and heavy that they needed a friend to help them lift the thing out of the back of a station wagon.

On the other hand, part of the fascination of getting involved in triathlons is that sleek, high-tech image. Nothing is going to give you that more than a good bike with all the fixin's. More to the point is that a lot of your hard work in certain areas is going to be wasted on the clunker—just as you would be hampered as a swimmer if you tried to train in one of those above-ground backyard pools.

The best advice, as always, is to play it smart. Know definitely what you want before you buy it. Start training with the best available equipment you can dig up cheaply, then invest in better when and if you decide to continue.

THE BASIC TRIATHLON BIKE

The best source of current information about cycling equipment is your local bike shop. But you need to get to the point where you can ask the right questions. So here are some guidelines:

You're looking for a lightweight (19–23 pounds) road-racing bike made of steel alloy tubing. Most aluminum or carbon-fiber frames will run the cost up astronomically—and needlessly. You don't need to get that fancy right off the bat. Most bikes in the $500 range have a good set of Japanese-made alloy components, certainly adequate for all the work you'll be doing for the first couple of years of triathlon training and racing. In fact, many cyclists prefer the top-of-the-line Japanese brands over the higher-priced Italian components—even when they can afford to pay the difference.

The fit of your bike is critical. Sore backs, stiff necks, and leg cramps—things that can actually take you out of a race—can come as a result of a bike that doesn't fit. And the tolerances are surprisingly small: a few centimeters one way or the other can make a big difference.

The rule of thumb is that when the frame is the right size for you, you should be able to stand flat-footed over the top tube—the tube that runs from the seat to the handlebars—and have about an inch of clearance below your crotch. But that's just a start. Stem height and handlebar width, the length of the crank arms, seat height, etc., etc., etc., all enter into the formula. There have been many good articles in the trade magazines about fitting your bike, but the only surefire method I know is to go to a good bike shop and have it done there. Some shops are better at it than others, of course, but trying to fit your bike yourself by reading about it in a book or in an article is tough.

The wheels are important, too. In fact, a good set of lightweight wheels can turn that clunker into a racing machine. There is a wide variety of wheels on the market, with a growing trend toward aerodynamic rims and spokes. What you should look for first is a pair of lightweight standard wheels that can be used for both training and racing. Once again, leave the fancy stuff for later, when you'll fully appreciate it. Do you really need to shave a minute off your best bike time in your first triathlon?

The wheels that will most likely come with your $500 bike will have clincher rims, made to be used with the kind of rubber tires you used as a kid—the kind that needed to be pried off the rim with little tools and had the tube inside. The new tires are thinner, though, and much lighter.

The other kind of rim you'll hear about is the tubular rim. It has less of a lip to hold the tire than the clincher rim, so the tire is attached with special cement. Tubular tires are also called "sew-ups." The tube, much thinner than a clincher tube, is actually sewn inside the tire. Tubular tires can be changed much more quickly on the road than clinchers—you just tear the tire off the rim and put another on—but they go flat more easily and patching them is a chore, so you end up spending a fortune on new tires.

Until you're ready for a separate set of wheels for racing (not now! not now!), stick with one-inch clinchers.

(A friend who has learned through hard, firsthand experience suggests that you might want to stick with clincher rims regardless, especially if you plan to do a lot of riding on long, steep hills. They're safer. Braking on the way down can actually heat the rim, and thus the glue, to a point where the glue softens and the tire either shifts or unseats itself altogether—not a pleasant matter at 30 or 40 or more miles an hour.)

The gearing on bicycles is not as mysterious as many people make it out to be. Your $500 bike will most likely come with ten speeds—two sets of gears on the crank, and five sets of gears on the back wheel, or the freewheel (5 × 2 = 10). The freewheel has a center portion that spins around as long as the wheel is moving, and an outer portion with gears that turns only when it's being pulled along by the chain. The crank gears usually have 42 and 52 teeth respectively; the freewheel cluster has cogs with the number of teeth ranging from 13 on up to 21 or 23.

Very simply, your bike is easiest to pedal when your chain is around the small (42 teeth) gear in front and the largest (21 or 23 teeth) in back. It's hardest to pedal when your chain is around the 52 in front and the 13 in back. Unless you plan to incorporate long-distance touring in the mountains into your triathlon training program, the 13-23 combination should suit most of your initial needs. (Most competitive triathletes have several rear clusters—which are interchangeable—so they can change gear ratios as particular courses demand.)

IF THE SHOE FITS

Once you become reasonably confident on the bike, once telephone poles and cars have become obstacles you can avoid without mashing your brakes, screaming in terror, and falling over, you should buy a pair of cycling shoes with cleats. You won't be able to learn the techniques of proper cycling without them. Competitive cycling shoes have rigid bottoms that translate all of the force of your downward stroke to the pedal without any of it getting lost in squishy padding. The cleats are grooved, designed to fit into the pedals, which have toe clips and straps attached to them. When the strap is drawn tight the foot is held firmly in place, so that you can pull up on the pedal as well as pushing down. Touring shoes—cycling shoes with a solid or semisolid plate under the ball of the foot but without the cleat—are a waste of time (assuming you don't own a pair already).

Cleats will come in the same box as your new cycling shoes, but they will come unmounted. They bolt into holes in the soles of the shoes. While installation is easy, proper

THE BIKE

positioning of the cleats is important. Poorly positioned cleats can lead quickly to injury by forcing your foot and leg to operate unnaturally. Another complication is that toe clips come in several lengths—too short and you won't be able to slide your foot far enough forward on the pedal; too long and you can place your cleat too far forward on the pedal.

Here's the basic principle: the ball of your foot should be *directly* over the center of the pedal, and your foot needs to sit on the pedal so that it doesn't force your ankle or knee out of alignment. Experiment on your indoor trainer or on the street before you tighten up the cleat screws. Make sure it's comfortable. A common way of doing it is to ride for several days, perhaps as long as a week, without the cleats. The pedal will wear a shallow groove in the sole of the shoe. Line up the slot in your cleat with that groove and tighten the screws. Pain on the inside or the outside of your knee is a good indication that you need to make some adjustments.

Cleats can be intimidating. You can't step out of the pedal by simply lifting your foot. Even experienced cyclists will occasionally pull to the top of a hill, forget that they haven't loosened a strap, and fall over. Remember the old "Laugh-In" routine with the guy in the rain slicker on the tricycle? It looks like that. Dumb.

Many recreational cyclists—indeed, many triathletes—avoid using cleats for that reason. They either ride in their sneakers or stop at the touring shoe level. You don't need to; you can get used to cleats if you just take things one step at a time. First, get used to your bike. Ride until you're well past the wobbly stage. Then ride with your cleats near your home, around the block, perhaps, but without pulling the straps tight. As you become more confident with that, gradually tighten the straps, one foot at a time. Do it all at a speed that's comfortable. Take a week. Take two. Or a month. Be patient. The investment will pay off. The cleats will help.

Note: There are several pedal systems on the market now

that do away with the clips and straps and lock the foot directly into the pedal. It's a good idea—the strap binding is often uncomfortable, and you can get out of the new systems more quickly, too. Ask at your bike shop.

WEAR A HELMET

Aside from the fact that approved hard-shell helmets are required in all triathlons in the United States, common sense dictates that you wear one during training, too. I know, I know, it's not part of the go-for-broke image, but neither is brain damage. Head injuries—serious head injuries—are common among cyclists, and most of the injuries are a result of going down with hair flying gloriously in the breeze. It isn't worth the risk. Cycling is dangerous enough. Besides, if you have to wear one in the race, why not get used to it?

CYCLING CLOTHING

The basic item here is a pair of cycling shorts, which in the old days came only in black, but now comes in about any color and pattern you could possibly imagine—and many you couldn't. Cycling shorts have an extended leg to prevent chafing on the saddle, and a padded crotch to prevent whatever you need to prevent down there.

Hard-shell helmets are required in triathlons. This is Mike Pigg of Arcata, California, looking his normal fierce self beneath an aerodynamic shell. If you're just beginning, be less concerned with speed and more concerned with something that's going to save your head in a crash.

Wearing underwear *and* padded cycling shorts is not recommended. The underwear will bunch and hike up and make you miserable. A friend of mine offers the additional suggestion that if you are going to ride in a pair of wild but light-colored cycling shorts, buy a seat cover, readily available at your local bike shop. Otherwise you might end up with unsightly black stains on your fashionable shorts.

While competitive triathlon wear is a matter of several choices that we'll discuss later, cycling shorts are still a standard item for training purposes.

In cool weather, lycra tights, again in all colors and patterns, have become the trademark of the triathlete, although to be honest, there are still some portions of the country where they aren't understood by the local nonathletes. You're on your own in that department. Wear your cycling shorts under the tights, so if the day warms up, you can remove the tights without *really* upsetting the neighbors. Besides, shorts worn over the tights look dumb.

On top, wear anything that's warm enough, makes you feel good, and doesn't flap a lot in the wind. Never underdress on a bike ride. Wear enough to stay warm in the worst conditions you can reasonably expect. Riding while you're cold is about the worst training experience you can have. You can actually end up hypothermic, wobbly in both mind and body, two things you do not want to be while riding a bike.

As far as cycling gloves go, their use in triathlons is limited; few athletes want to bother taking the time to put them on and take them off in the transition area, so many learn to train without them, too. However, gloves can make your training more comfortable and help you avoid numb fingers and hands. They also can make a big difference if you fall. Whatever you feel most comfortable with is the way to go.

CAN'T SEE THE FOREST FOR THE SHADES

Sunglasses are a big help. They not only keep you from squinting, they keep bugs and dirt out of your eyes. There

Shades, like tights, have become a part of the triathlon culture. They help when you're on the road, too. Might as well be fashionable.

are several brands that are a part of the triathlon scene, so if you're going to invest, you might as well take a look at *Triathlete* magazine before you do and see what's what. Whatever you buy, get something with temples that hook behind your ears or wear a strap of some kind. Nothing worse than bouncy glasses.

BASIC TECHNIQUE

Your main obstacle to riding fast is unseen, although hardly unfelt. It's the air—wind resistance. Even on a calm day, most of the cyclist's energy is spent overcoming wind resistance. And the faster you go the worse it gets. Highly competitive triathletes spend thousands of dollars (sponsor dollars, usually) on the latest innovations in aerodynamic equipment so they can shave seconds off their bike times. "Funny bikes," with curved tubing and dropped front ends, small front wheels, aero rims and spokes, disc wheels, aero handlebars, internal cable systems, and on and on, can in fact make a difference in total time between riders of equal ability unequally equipped.

But you know what works best? Good legs. Dave Scott made a lot of people sit back and smile when he demolished the field at the 1986 Ironman on a basic machine. Everyone else was super high-tech; Scott was just super high-tough.

The new equipment is terrific, really. But there are a lot of mediocre triathletes riding around on $2,000 bikes who could get faster if they just learned how to sit and pedal correctly on something $1,500 cheaper. Start with the basics and work up as your knowledge and ability increase.

"I'm a great believer in the idea that it's your *body*, not your bike, that makes the biggest difference," says 1985 Ironman champ Joanne Ernst. "Better to train your body than spend tons of money trying to shave off a second here or there. Plus, much of the aerodynamic equipment is not especially reliable. In triathlon you're on your own if your bike breaks down."

Efficiency on the hills is important. Note the cyclist on the right. He's in good position: low, with his weight over the pedals. The cyclist on the left is pulling up, away from where she needs to go—much too much arm, not enough leg.

Racing position on the bike. You'll go fastest when your hands are in the drops. Keep your back flat, your body as low as possible. Don't hold your head up too high; look where you're going by peeking up from underneath the edge of your helmet.

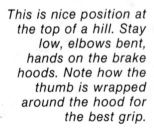

This is nice position at the top of a hill. Stay low, elbows bent, hands on the brake hoods. Note how the thumb is wrapped around the hood for the best grip.

BODY POSITION

Simple. Stay low. Keep your knees and elbows in and stay low. Cut the wind resistance, remember? Also, put the center of your cycling power constantly over the pedals. The more directly your weight is over the scene of the action, the better.

Your arms should be bent and relaxed. Most beginning cyclists put too much weight on their arms. They lean on their hands, which not only takes power away from the legs but tires their arms as well. Don't bend forward to get low, squish down.

There are two positions most frequently used in triathlon training and competition: hands on the lower, curved portion of the handlebars (or "drops"); and hands resting on the brake hoods, with the thumb to the inside, toward the stem, and the middle of your index finger bearing the weight on the outside. The second position is the most comfortable for training; the first is more frequently seen in races. Learn to be happy in both. During a triathlon the best strategy is to shift from one to the other to minimize stiffness and fatigue.

In both positions try to keep your back as flat as possible. Look up at the road from underneath the rim of your helmet; don't hold your head up high—you'll get a stiff neck. Practice maintaining a streamlined posture on every ride. It will feel awkward at first, but not forever.

A third position puts both hands in front of you around the straight part of the handlebars. This is a seated position only, more of an alternative to the hands-on-the-brake-hoods position than anything else; it's used frequently when climbing long hills. It's perfectly acceptable. Stay low here, too.

DON'T PUSH A GOOD THING TOO FAR

In fact, try not to push at all—on your pedals. The correct word here is "spin." Contrary to what you might think, the emphasis should not be on pushing down or pulling up, but rather on a combination of both. The technically correct cyclist turns his or her pedals at a rate of 75 to 100 times a minute. The laborious, plunging, up-and-down action you may have seen on the road—a cyclist with his back bouncing and his feet jabbing—is simply a matter of poor technique.

The best way to practice spinning is on an indoor trainer, which is one of the reasons I included it on the basic equipment list at the beginning of the chapter. An indoor trainer is a stationary platform for your bicycle that uses a small turbine fan to simulate wind resistance. (The trainers are sometimes called wind-load simulators.) Just as resistance will increase on the road as you move faster, so does resistance on the trainer increase as you pedal harder. Spinning can also be practiced on the road, of course—it's just easier to get distracted.

First of all, to get an idea of how much you *don't* spin, put your bike in low gear (easier to pedal) and try pedaling with one leg. (If you're on the road, just relax with one leg—let the other one do all the work.) If you're like most people, the pushing down part will feel natural, but the pulling up part will feel ridiculous. Trying to turn the pedal *around* the center of the crank is even worse. But in fact, that's the goal: turning smooth, continuous circles. One good way to think of how this works is to try to "feel" the chain. (I'm speaking figuratively, of course. A friend suggested that I warn you not to try to reach down and actually *do* that. How painful!) Anyway, you should concentrate on keeping the chain moving smoothly around the big chain ring, without a break or hesitation of any sort in your pedaling action. If you're working on an indoor trainer, you'll not only feel when this happens, you'll hear it. The turbine fans make a lot of noise; when you're applying equal force to your entire pedal stroke, their sound is a nice, steady whoosh.

To cement the technique of spinning, you need to ride frequently in low gears, keeping your pedaling rate in the range of 75–100 times a minute. Eighty-five is just about right. Determining your rpms is easy: check your watch

An aerodynamic position coming down steep hills is fast, but it destabilizes the bike. You need to know what you're doing, so be careful. This is Scott Molina at a race in Denver. I was in the press truck he's passing at this point—he's moving almost 60 miles an hour.

and count the number of times your right knee comes up in one minute. Riding in high gears all the time—pedaling more slowly—might make you feel you're getting a better workout, but you'll never learn to spin that way, and you run the risk of injuring your knees.

Watch the knees on the hills, too. Spinning applies when you are climbing, just as it does when you're on the flats. Keep the rotations high. Grinding away, pushing and pushing and pushing, is not only inefficient, it'll lead to

97

injury. And it's slow. In most cases, you're a lot faster in your seat than you are standing up, so stay there whenever possible and keep the pedals turning.

MOVING DOWN AND AROUND

You've probably seen cyclists in some strange positions when coming down a steep hill. Almost all of the positions make the bike unstable, and are not the kind of thing a beginner needs to try. If you're moving so fast that you can't pedal without bouncing all over your seat, it's time to coast. Shift your hands into the drops and squeeze your body tight, with your elbows and knees in, but don't lose sight of the road. Wait until you gain skill, confidence, and a friend who knows how before you try to get fancy. Always brake gently before a downhill corner, not during. Play this safe, too, until you know what you're doing. Stay loose and keep your weight centered over the bike. Anticipate problems and stay within your ability level, and if you decide to extend yourself a little, commit fully and then go for it. Desperately not wanting to fall is a great way to do just that. So is changing your mind in the middle of a tight spot.

FIND A KNOWLEDGEABLE PARTNER

The best way to learn how to ride is to ride, and the more people you can ride with who know what they're doing, the better. That's a problem, of course, if you're a beginner—too slow to stay up with anyone you think is good. But there are ways around that. Cyclists have a reputation for being on the snooty side and not very helpful, but they're not all like that. Certainly, triathletes aren't, and not every group of experienced riders goes hard all the time. In San Diego, for instance, the famous Wednesday ride north to Dana Point is pretty much a social affair on the way up (it's hell on the way back, though). Many nonelite riders go for part of the ride north and learn from the best—without being made to feel stupid or having to drag themselves home totally exhausted.

TRAINING

Cycling is something you need to get good at—and something that you can get better at by simply doing. Spend as much time as possible on your bike. Ride to work, ride to the store, ride to and from swim practice. Take your bike on errands whenever possible. Don't worry at first about quality as much as just getting used to sitting in the seat.

Bike safety is critical. Quite simply, cycling is dangerous, and if you don't hit the road with that thought in mind, then you might have to hit the road to be reminded. Please use caution. Stop at stop signs and stoplights. Signal when you're about to move anywhere but straight ahead in traffic. By no means ride in the dark or even at dusk if you can avoid it, and don't take the helmet off until you're safely home or wherever you're going.

Triathletes and cyclists have a tendency to get careless when they're training. They tend to get aggressive and take stupid chances, to act as if the road belongs to them. But the exact opposite is true: it belongs to the people driving cars, whether you agree with them or not.

Your normal training course should be on well-paved roads with wide shoulders and as little traffic as possible. Varied terrain—a combination of flats and hills—is best. As you come to know the course better you'll be able to read your gradual improvement easily: the hills will seem flatter, the entire route more manageable. Keep track of your times in your training log, and after you graduate to longer rides, return to the original course to gauge your progress.

You'll find that having a steady, dependable route is convenient. There may be times when it's boring, but other times—when you're pressured to get in a workout before dashing off to another obligation—when the familiarity will be welcome.

Where interval training sharply defines the parameters of your swimming training, the training format on the bike is more relaxed, which is good on one end, but can lead to stagnation once that first thrust of rapid improvement has peaked. Here are a couple of alternatives:

Group rides are a good idea for a beginning cyclist in any case. There's so much to learn about the sport, and while you may be intimidated at first by the technical atmosphere of a bike shop, you can watch and learn from better riders during a ride without asking a single question. There's an obvious benefit in training with cyclists who are stronger and faster than you are.

Group rides, however, can be dangerous. One cyclist who makes an error in judgment can bring the whole gang down in a second. "Pace-lining"—one cyclist close behind another behind another and so on—is how groups usually ride, but if you're not confident of your bike-handling ability, stay back a bit. Give yourself some room for error.

When you're riding in a group, never allow your front wheel to overlap the rear wheel of another cyclist, and never make quick movements to one side or another without taking a look. Stay clear of road hazards. Point them out to cyclists riding behind you.

Varying your pace during a ride accomplishes the same thing that intervals do in swimming. Every few days attack the hills more aggressively than usual, or try doing segments of the ride at a faster pace, slowing down afterward to catch your breath, then speeding through a section farther up the road. Don't speed up drastically—increase your pace just 10 percent or so, and hold the new pace for 10 to 15 minutes.

Sprinting for street signs is a technique many cyclists use to make group rides more entertaining and challenging. It works exactly the way it sounds—exactly the way it might if one kid challenged another to race for a big tree in the backyard. Make sure you're warmed up thoroughly before you get into this stuff, though. You can easily blow a knee or a hamstring. And don't be so intent on getting there first that you forget safety.

While sprinting will hardly be of use to you in triathlons, maintaining good leg speed is important—training tends to be not only specific in terms of a particular sport, it is specific too in terms of pace. The only way to ride a little faster is to train a little faster.

Long rides, 25 to 100 percent (and more) longer than your average ride, are an important part of a cycling training program. Usually, long rides are done on weekends, when you're not pressed for time. Long rides can be daunting at first, but they can become the highlight of your week. Pick a destination, pick a couple of training partners, bring money, food, and plenty of water, and you can turn the day into an adventure.

Cycling indoors on your trainer can be a crashing bore, and I'm not really sure how to get around that. The turbine fans make a good deal of noise, so you've got to crank the volume of the television or stereo way up. Small price, though—without something visual or aural to keep you alert, the trainer is death.

The nice part about indoor training is that it's efficient. The man who developed one of the early models claimed that a half hour on the trainer was worth a full hour on the road. And as I've already mentioned, it's great for smoothing out your technique. Many top triathletes use the trainer regularly to isolate one leg—first the left, then the right. Mark Allen, five-time winner of the Nice Triathlon, has said that he can handle 20 minutes on each leg. Seeing him ride, you'd believe that, but it's an incredible feat. Try just five yourself. I'll bet you don't make it.

You'll also notice in your training how much you sweat when you ride. Without any breeze to evaporate the perspiration, it really pours. You'll corrode your machine if you don't cover the base with towels. An alternative to drowning is to set up a fan in front of your trainer. If you're going to be noisy, might as well go all out.

Even when the weather permits riding outdoors, a weekly session on the trainer will do your cycling a lot of good. It won't be the most enjoyable part of your training, but it'll be one of the most productive.

When to train—Bad weather makes scheduling your

Check your equipment carefully before the race. Sometimes even the most careful precautions are no help, but carelessness is a sure way to an unhappy finish.

cycling more complicated than swimming or running. If at all possible, it's best to ride after you swim to maximize the swim-to-bike adaptation—even if you swim in the morning and don't ride until after work. What you want to avoid at all costs is riding in rush-hour traffic. As I've already mentioned, you can make the most of your time by riding at every available opportunity, including to and from work.

COMPETITION

The bike ride is the fulcrum of a triathlon, the point on which your race will balance—or not. Carelessness on the bike in the areas of pacing or safety or logistics can negate a lot of hard work. We'll take the competition one step at a time:

1. Make sure your bike is in good mechanical condition, your tires without cuts. If you're not sure of your own skills as a mechanic, have your bike checked by a shop you've dealt with before—and have it checked soon enough so that you can ride a day or two before the race. That way any loose screws or missing pieces can be taken care of. I got real cocky about my mechanical ability and overhauled my bike the night before a race in 1983. Had a great race the next day, except that I'd left a washer off one of the crank arms, so the bolt holding it on kept loosening up. The whole arm actually fell off twice. I kept having to stop and tighten the bolt with my fingers. When I did, of course, people that I'd passed back up the road would go by. I must have passed this one guy six or seven times in the course of a 50-mile ride. It was a great psychological ploy; it destroyed him. He couldn't figure out what I was doing. But then, neither could I.

The moral of the story is to road test your bike before a competition if you insist on doing the work yourself.

Five-time Ironman Dave Scott just off his bike. This is a good shot of the organized transition areas of the best triathletes in an international-distance race—everything is laid out neatly on a towel, ready to go. The solid rear wheels are aerodynamic discs, which are quite expensive, hardly something a beginner needs to even think about.

Out of the swim, off on the bike. Even beginners can have a lot of fun refining their transition technique. You can get faster in triathlon simply by getting better at the little things.

2. *Make a checklist the night before the race of things you need to bring to the race.* Then *use* the list on race morning. Can you imagine trying to cycle 25 miles with one shoe?

3. *Set up your transition area with your mind set firmly on what is most likely to go wrong.* Set your bike in a gear that's easy to pedal before you head out for the swim. Make sure the laces of your shoes are untied. Where is your bike located? Your first triathlon is likely to have hundreds of people in it. Some landmarks will really help.

4. *After the swim, take your time.* Take a deep breath. Be sure, instead of fast and sloppy—being sure will probably make you quicker in the long run anyway. As in the swim, ignore the crowd. If you need to make a choice—and almost everyone does—it's better to look like Greg LeMond on the way in rather than on the way out.

5. *This is a triathlon, remember? Three sports.* Cycling tends to be a real ego thing. You can get so caught up in racing to the death during the ride, only to find that the muscles in your legs have turned to gray goo when it comes time for the run. Pacing is important. As a beginner your mission in the triathlon world is to finish your first couple of races and learn something. Crossing the finish line on hands and knees is a bad way to learn.

Drafting is illegal in triathlons, and is a major source of controversy in the sport. The Tri-Fed rules are specific: you cannot be within two bike lengths behind or three feet to one side of another triathlete unless you are passing. You have 15 seconds to complete the pass—to put your wheel in front of the other person.

At most triathlons there are marshals on motorcycles whose job it is to enforce the no-drafting rules with either

Drafting is not allowed during the bike ride. The rules say that you can't be within two bike lengths behind another rider or three feet to one side unless you are passing. You have 15 seconds to make the pass. A cyclist can gain a tremendous advantage by drafting—both in terms of speed gained and energy conserved.

penalties or disqualifications. Unfortunately, it's become a rare event in which no one is penalized. Triathletes at the 1986 Bud Light USTS National Championship didn't take prerace warnings seriously enough and 10 percent of the field of 1,500 ended up with penalties. Dumb.

Beyond the issue of ethics, riding close to the other cyclists in a triathlon is asking for trouble. It's bad enough in training, when a bad bump or a lapse in attention can send a whole group of riders down. But in a race, with people of unproven bike-handling ability all around you, the risks are too high.

(Personally, I'd rather see drafters painted red than disqualified. Drafting is cheating, pure and simple. Ruins the sport. If you see someone drafting in your first race, take a bite out of his leg. I'll buy you a beer.)

Special competitive apparel for triathlons takes several forms, although the current trend is toward simplicity. The *tri-suit*—a tight-fitting, one-piece suit designed to be worn in all three events—is the most popular option. At least for women. Men competing in international-distance races are leaning toward the simplest solution of all—the nylon or lycra swimsuit for the swim, bike, and run. Modesty used to dictate that a pair of nylon running shorts be worn for the last event, but that feeling is fading. Chafing during the bike ride is minimized with vaseline, either applied to the inside of thighs before the swim, or a gob placed underneath the bicycle seat, which can be spread around during the ride itself.

If you're a man with the body or the mind—or both—to get through the whole race with just a swimsuit, I recommend it. Saves time, and who needs an extra piece of clothing to worry about?

It's unlikely that novice triathletes are going to be worried about shaving off precious seconds during their first few races. I've made several previous references to that being unnecessary. On the other hand, where cost and long experience are not prerequisites, moving forward with the state of the sport can't hurt, and can make competition a lot

Scott Molina, arguably the best short and middle-distance triathlete in the world since 1982. This is a funny shot of him crossing the finish line, with his tongue out and all, but check the legs. If yours look like this, you really have no need to worry about what people will say if you keep them shaved.

more fun. (Proficiency—regardless of speed—is something all of us can enjoy.)

Shaving your legs. Speaking of shaving . . . this is a big step for some men. Bold. Devil-may-care. I get a kick out of

Keep your head up and your eyes open when coming back into the transition area on your bike. This is one of the most dangerous parts of the whole race. Here is 1985 Bud Light USTS National Champion Linda Buchanan.

some of the men triathletes in San Diego who don't give their shaved legs a thought—that and wearing pink, zebra-striped tights. A few years ago they were doing nothing but running marathons and would have dropped dead at the idea of being seen in public in something like that. "Shave my legs?! Are you *crazy*?"

Well, times change. Competitive cyclists have shaved their legs for years. So now do many triathletes. Aside from the fact that it's sleek and aerodynamic, having your legs shaved will keep road rash (patches of scraped skin) suffered in a fall less likely to be jammed with hair and become infected. Mostly, having your legs shaved facilitates massage, which cyclists employ religiously and which runners have largely ignored—in my mind much to their detriment.

If you can afford it, I'd recommend a regular program (once a week) of massage administered by a professional, a sports massage therapist. It will speed up recovery between workouts tremendously.

Beyond that, shaved legs have become the fashion in the triathlon world. I had to let you know, anyway.

Drinking fluids on the bike is something all competitors need to be conscious of. Because you're moving quickly you're often not aware of how much fluid you're losing. It often seems cooler than it really is, and the wind is drying perspiration before you can notice it. Don't rely on the aid stations at triathlons—sometimes they're good, sometimes not. Carry at least one full water bottle onto the bike course. Attaching a spare bottle cage is a snap, so I'd take two bottles along just to make sure. Failure to drink enough during the bike is going to come back to haunt you during the run.

OPTIONAL EQUIPMENT

This could fill a whole book in itself, but it would be a little like telling someone the outcome of a murder mystery in advance. Walking into a bike shop all goggled-eyed and discovering the latest gear is half the fun. There are some items that are actually useful:

Bicycle computer—These mount on your handlebars and are connected to your wheel by a variety of mechanisms. They can keep track of your mileage, pace per mile, rpms and more. They're a big help—many top triathletes and cyclists use them all the time, even in races. The simpler, less-ambitious models are probably the best.

Bicycle traveling case—If you plan to do any traveling by air with your bike, a case is almost a must. The standard cardboard bike boxes the airlines offer are an invitation to disaster. That old luggage commercial on television that showed a gorilla handling baggage was not far off the mark.

Several varieties of bike cases are available; you trade off for size with having more work to do in putting your bike back together.

Standing bicycle pump—The standard, hand-action frame pumps that come with your bike can be a pain, especially on the morning of a race. A good, heavy-duty pump is a great investment. The only drawback is that everyone will want to borrow the stupid thing.

Cold weather gloves—There are several kinds made especially for cyclists. These are not the standard, training-type cycling gloves with no fingers, but full, five-fingered gloves for cold November mornings. There are days when gloves are as essential as your front wheel.

Fanny pack—Handy for carrying your wallet, a wind-breaker, tights, an extra spare tire, etc., etc. Just make sure you put the pack on right side up. A friend of mine used one at the Ironman a couple of years back, turned it around to the front, unzipped it, and everything fell out onto the road. Good move.

INJURIES

Overuse injuries are relatively common on the bike. As you might expect, the knees are the weak spot. Improper biomechanical alignment due to poor cleat placement can be a cause of knee pain early in your training. So can pushing high gears. Grinding along constantly at rpms lower than 60 to 70 is tough on the legs. Avoid it.

Sore spots that develop during training can be treated with ice, applied with steady pressure for about 20 minutes after each workout. Elevate your leg when applying the ice.

There's no good rule of thumb as to when you should see an orthopedist. Pain is one key: if your knee is sore when you start to ride, but warms up and gives you no problem from then on, lay off the hills for a while, maybe take a few days off, and keep icing regularly. It's probably something you can handle.

On the other hand, if the pain doesn't go away, or if it gets worse, or if it gets worse as you continue to ride, then you probably should seek help. Don't be a hero, there's no future in it.

One precaution you can take is to wear tights in cool weather. Cold muscles and tendons are easier to injure than warm ones. Your Achilles tendon—the long one at the back of your heel—is especially vulnerable. It is, after all (sorry about this), your Achilles' heel.

International-distance triathlons can get exciting. Mike Pigg and New Zealander Richard Wells gave the crowd a thrill as they battled for second place at the USTS race in Dana Point, California, in 1986.

6
THE RUN

The competitive goal: 6.2 miles
  The training goal: 8–10 miles
    Basic equipment: pair of running shoes ($40–$90)

Running is the simplest of the three triathlon events, but it carries the greatest risk of overuse injury. Newcomers to running with recent experience as either cyclists or swimmers might find themselves capable of running acceptable distances almost immediately, but are equally capable of going too far too fast. As one champion cyclist-turned-triathlete described it, "Swimmers and cyclists tend to have soft legs."

A solid base of cardiovascular fitness is a blessing, but it needs to be used wisely.

For people moving into triathlon from a running background there is a hidden problem, too. Training in three sports, former full-time runners usually find it impossible to maintain their previous level of running mileage. They feel bad about that, perhaps even guilty. The time con-

113

straints are real, the workouts in the other two sports are tiring, still . . . The guilt then leads to either overtraining or a lack of enthusiasm for maintaining necessary levels in swimming or cycling.

The answer to both problems is simple. The sport of triathlon needs to be seen as just that, a sport—with its own credibility. It requires a delicate balance of three elements, each playing successfully off the others for the maximum benefit of all. If the running is rushed along, injury will result, and the other two areas will suffer. If a mileage reduction is something you only grudgingly accept, perhaps it's best that you run, although, quite frankly, you'll never run well in a triathlon unless you pay attention to your swimming and cycling. "Waiting for my best event" is a commonly heard but ever-failing strategy that runners new to the triathlon often voice. By the time their "best event" arrives, they usually find themselves being passed by grandmothers and 12-year-old boys in tennis sneakers.

Curiously, the best of all worlds is to be a good athlete but never to have had any formal experience in either running, swimming, or cycling. That way you can train as a triathlete from the beginning without any preconceptions. As the sport of triathlon becomes more firmly established, many people are doing just that.

BASIC TECHNIQUE

Don't try to make any drastic changes in your natural running style. A lot of "poor form" is a matter of poor conditioning, or of individual body construction. Distance running is much more tolerant of bad technique than most other sports. Forcing yourself to run like Sebastian Coe or Carlos Lopes is just going to lead to injury or frustration or both. While it's unlikely that you can tell at first glance how the styles of the top cyclists on the Tour de France differ, the differences in style between the world's top marathoners is striking, obvious to even the unpracticed eye. With neither aerodynamics nor aquadynamics to worry about, runners improve mostly by maximizing their fitness level instead of matching their running style to an idealized norm.

(The best example of this is Dave Scott, five-time winner of the Ironman, and the man who has run the marathon stage of that race more than 10 minutes faster than anyone. His 2:49 Ironman best—after a 50-minute swim and a 4:48 bike ride—is nothing short of spectacular. His running style, however, is far from classic. A mutual friend calls him "The World's Fastest Duck.")

Which doesn't mean that improving your technique won't help, but it does mean you can play with it gently and gradually. Try different foot placements and stride lengths and breathing until you find a combination that works best for you. What you're most likely to discover is that different solutions work well on different days. There are no magical answers.

The proper running shoe, however, *is* critical. The vast amount of research and development in the running shoe industry over the last decade has resulted in a confusing array of choices. Knowing the different brands is not nearly enough, for each company makes shoes for several different kinds of runners. Fitting your own style into the puzzle is important. Do you strike the ground first with your forefoot or your heel? Are you a *pronator* (feet roll to the inside when they strike) or a *supinator* (feet roll to the outside)? What physiological factors—like arch height and foot width—affect your running?

The only way to find the answers to these questions is, of course, to run. If you're an experienced runner, nothing I've said is new. If you're a novice, however, you may want to reexamine the shoes you've been running in. If they look pretty beat up, or if they really weren't designed for more than an occasional jog to the store, it wouldn't hurt to celebrate the beginning of your triathlon training by going out and buying a new pair. Look at the wear pattern on the soles of the ones you've been wearing. That will tell you what part of your foot you land on and how your foot

The toughest part of any triathlon for most people is running after a hard bike ride. At the Ironman, they complicate things by starting the full marathon with a huge hill. Feels just fine after cycling 112 miles in the lava fields, you know?

responds to the impact. Read the latest *Runner's World* shoe survey, then head for the best running shoe specialty shop you can find and ask a lot of questions. Walk out with something you are completely satisfied with.

As a triathlete, the broadest technical goal for your running is to *stay relaxed*. Being stylish is less important than being efficient. Alberto Salazar has shuffled successfully through some rather fast marathons. Keep your shoulders high but not pulled back, and your posture erect but not stiff. That will facilitate your breathing. Push through your stride with your toes. "Run from your hips," is a piece of advice that's been around a long time, and it's a good one. When you're running well, it does indeed feel as if your entire body is moving along in one piece, right from the center.

Since running comes last in a triathlon, you'll need to become an expert at running when you're tired. Concentrate hard during those last couple of miles. Experiment constantly. Assemble a catalog of technical changes and mental tricks you can call on during a race, because you'll never know what's going to work until you get there. Head position, arm swing, breathing, foot plant—almost anything can make a difference. Over the years I've talked with many top triathletes who stumbled through the run at the Ironman only to find out with five miles to go that what made them feel better was actually to speed up rather than slow down. Don't ever be afraid to try something that *shouldn't* work.

Once again, stay relaxed. A lot of tension builds up when you get tired, especially in your upper body, neck, and face. Not only does the tension waste energy but it restricts blood flow to your lower extremities, where it's needed the most.

In the latter stages of a tough run, your shoulders and hips tend to droop and your head wobbles. Be aware of these changes and try to minimize them in your training. The trick is to feel as if you are running the same way at the end as you were at the beginning—mechanically at least. That you *feel* like you're about to have your third child is beside the point.

One specific suggestion: if you run with a naturally long stride, you might want to shorten it slightly. Your legs are going to be tight at the end of the bike ride and you'll find it impossible to stretch out right away.

You're supposed to finish, that's all. You're not supposed to look like you've just played a set of doubles tennis.

TRAINING

Running is the easiest of the three sports to schedule, since you need neither great weather nor daylight. (A friend reminds me that running in the dark might not be such a great idea. She's right. Use your head. A woman should probably never run alone at night—for obvious reasons—and regardless of which sex you are, run only where the streets are well-lit so you won't turn an ankle in a hole or crack you didn't see.)

On the other hand, running is the easiest of the three sports to goof off on. Don't shove it aside "for later." Some triathletes do. Find out where your cycling and swimming need to be, then carve a regular niche for running and leave it there.

"Don't get so seduced by this sexy new sport and all the sexy new technology that you ease off on your running skills," warns one top Masters triathlete who did just that.

Running can anchor your whole triathlon conditioning program, since you can run from almost anywhere—work, an airport, after a meeting, whatever. If traveling or a temporary business situation cuts into the rest of your training, gradually increase your running to compensate.

Most of your running mileage will probably be over a familiar route at a distance you feel consistently comfortable with. Your experience and schedule will determine exactly how far. Four to six miles is common. As with your cycling, time yourself occasionally over your standard route to gauge your progress.

Once a week you should do a long run—up to twice your normal distance. The pace hardly matters; the idea behind the extra miles is to get your body used to staying in motion for an extended period of time. For marathoners, the weekly long run—from 20 to 30 miles—is critical. Among other things, it lets their bodies adapt chemically to the long periods of stress, refining the process of energy flow and utilization.

For the beginning triathlete whose long run may be only

8 to 10 miles, it's unlikely that the physiological adaptation is as pronounced as for the marathoner. Still, it occurs. Perhaps even more important, the weekly long run will greatly increase your confidence. Do your long run at a slow, comfortable pace; don't race.

Just to give you an idea of how these things go, here's how one triathlete I know described a five-mile fartlek run over varying terrain:

Warmup, 1.5 miles—"From the front door I ease into my run, jogging a little, taking a couple of real deep breaths to get my lungs working. By the time I've gone a half-mile or so, I'm into my normal training pace. I turn right onto the sidewalk of the main street and run halfway down a long hill. I make a point of bouncing over a fire hydrant there—one foot on top and then over. Puts me in the mood. About 50 yards past the hydrant I turn right onto a dirt road, which drops off very quickly and steeply."

Fast-paced, 1 mile—"As I reach the bottom of the hill, I let fly a little and push hard into a steep, short uphill. I concentrate here on shortening my stride, keeping my arms high, and pushing strongly off my toes. I try to anticipate my need to breathe hard by setting the rhythm right away. When I crest the hill I give it a little added jolt coming over the top, then let myself float down the other side. The terrain is rough here, very rocky, and I have fun picking my way down. Then there's another hill like the first. This whole mile is steep ups and downs—I get so wrapped up in working hard and trying not to fall on my face, I forget that I'm tired."

Jog, 400 yards—"As the ground levels off a bit, I slow into a jog. I'm breathing hard at this point. There are a couple of spots that are boggy, and I have to tiptoe around them, which slows me down even more. A quarter-mile later, when I turn off the dirt road onto a little footpath, my breathing has returned to normal."

Fast again, 400 yards—"The terrain gets bad on the footpath as it comes up and over a set of railroad tracks, then leads me down over an area where erosion has cut deep tracks in the dirt. Then there's a deep cut with a little stream at the bottom. I go down that and up the bank on the other side, where it's almost like a steep set of stairs. At the top I follow the path to the left through some head-high underbrush—I have to duck under and around that. I can barely see the path at all. Finally there's a sharp little rise where the path intersects with the main trail at the bottom of the canyon. I turn right on the trail and jog. I'm usually breathing real hard at this point, but I'm having fun with it, too."

Ease back to normal pace, 800 yards—"The trail is wide and flat through the canyon. It's pretty here. In the late afternoon there are rabbits all over the place and hawks soaring overhead. I take my time and run easily, letting my breathing settle down. I run across an old wooden bridge and then turn right, back toward the railroad tracks. As the path slopes up slightly I start to pick up the pace again."

Build to hard effort, 1 mile—"Usually there are two wires strung to keep vehicles off the trail—one before the tracks and one just after. I hurdle both of these, then push up a short, steep embankment, all of which gets my breathing going again. At the top of the embankment there's a 180-degree turn to a sidewalk. I hold the pace here, but since the footing is firm, my breathing comes back down. I continue to force the pace just slightly for the next mile or so. This is a long, steady, curving climb that gets slightly steeper at the top. If I've gone extra hard in the middle of the run, or I feel a little off, it can get real tough here. If I'm feeling good, I try to *make* it be tough. Finally, at the top there's a right turn where I ease off and head for home. The last half-mile is relaxed."

A more formal alternative to a fartlek run is one in which you press your normal speed for specific periods of time: one minute, two minutes, etc. This is a good way to develop a sense of pace and also to feel around the edges of what a race is like. Punch the timer on your watch and speed up just slightly. Accelerate to a steady pace within 25 yards or so, then hold it at that. A problem many beginners have is speeding up and speeding up and speeding up until they're ready to fall over.

RACING IS THE BEST TRAINING FOR RACING

If your first triathlon is also your first experience in a mass-participation athletic event, you're going to be carrying an unnecessary psychological burden. Local 10K or 5K running races are terrific training for triathletes. Not only will they take some of the edge off your inexperience, they will give you an opportunity to test your sense of pace and your level of fitness. Beyond that, they are proving grounds for small things that will loom large on T-Day: shoes and clothing, what to eat before a race, and what kind of prerace warmup works best for you.

Approach local races informally. Enjoy them. Gauge the results by how much you've learned, not by how you've placed. Get used to the competitive environment.

Coming down toward the finish line, with the sound of the crowd in your ears, you'll often find yourself able to do more with your body than you thought possible.

SPORTSPERFORMANCE

RUNNING AFTER YOUR BIKE RIDE

Even if you're a terrific runner, this is liable to shock you. In fact, it might shock you *more* if you're a terrific runner. The feeling is probably something like what Frankenstein's monster encountered the first time he walked away from the laboratory table—same old brain, someone else's legs. Ugh!

There's only one way to get used to the feeling: you need to run after you ride. Some people believe you shouldn't do this frequently because the risk of injury is too great. My feeling is that since the pace at first is going to be little better than a crawl, it hardly matters.

After your first month of triathlon training, make it a point to jog no more than a mile or two after three bike rides a week. Don't push. Not only will you be giving your body a chance to adjust, you'll feel your mind adapt, too. Learn not to panic over how things feel at first. Be patient. Your legs will indeed "come back to you," and they'll come back faster and faster with practice.

Following the first few weeks of experimentation, set one day a week aside for a real run—four, five miles at the most—after a 15-to-25-mile bike ride. It probably won't feel too great—you even may be reduced to walking stretches the first time—but stay with it. Of all the training exercises that will help you get through your first triathlon in good shape, this is perhaps the most important. Make a point of not running the next day—give your body a chance to recover.

(I'd like to add a little encouragement here. Moving from the bike to the run is a strange experience for almost everyone. I've seen good runners experiencing it for the first time just stop and laugh. You do get better at it with time.)

When to train. As I've already mentioned, running is the easiest of the three sports to schedule; almost any time is a good time. But you might want to try to run as often as possible at a time of day when you are most likely to be running in competition. Run occasionally in the late morning or afternoon to get used to the heat.

122

Kirsten Hanssen saves time in the bike/run transition area by carrying her number with her as she goes. She'll put it on during the run.

Mike Pigg, a top pro triathlete, is on the ground, changing shoes, with cyclists coming in from the bike course.

COMPETITION

Moving from the bike ride to the run in a triathlon isn't physically complicated—it's certainly the simpler of the two transitions—but it can be strategically confusing. Your mind needs to be in control of the situation at this point, not your body, and certainly not your emotions. Take the change one step at a time:

1. Think. Where's your bike rack? Start mapping out your transition while you're still in the saddle. There's going to be a lot of movement and a lot of screaming and yelling when you get into the transition area.

2. Come in slowly. Keep your head up and your eyes open as you enter the transition area. Don't be a hero. Riding in from the bike course can be a real psych-up, and

I've seen cyclists push the last 400 yards faster than they pushed the rest of the ride—then go down in a painful heap.

3. Go smoothly. Panic is only going to waste energy you'll need later. Rack your bike, then sit and switch shoes. Some people stand and change, but your legs aren't going to be quite steady after the ride; it's better to sit. After your laces are tight, stand and pull on any clothes you're going to wear. Now make sure you know where you're going. Which way is the course? Flying off blindly can mean either running into a bike just coming in or running off in the wrong direction. Smooth, remember?

Here's the best way to go for the women: bathing suit, number on a strip of elastic fabric pulled over the head or from the feet up. Off the bike and go!

Triathletes need to be experts in the art of keeping themselves well hydrated during competition. Nothing can stop you faster—and harder—than dehydration. Alison Roe, of marathon fame, heads out of the bike/run transition area of the race in Phoenix paying strict attention to her basic needs.

4. Start running slowly. Use short strides and let your pace develop. Grab water on your way out. Don't miss that first aid station, whatever you do. Make a point of ignoring the fools who blast out of the transition area looking like Carl Lewis. You'll probably see them again four miles down the road, and you'll be able to give them a pat on the butt as you go by.

5. Take aid at every opportunity. Never miss a water stop. Keep yourself wet outside and in. Hyperthermia (overheating) is a danger every triathlete needs to be aware of.

DEALING WITH THE HEAT

Most triathlons take place during the summer. The

season in the United States is usually April–September. Although the races start early—7 A.M. or so—by the time you get off your bike the sun is high and hot. Dehydration and rising internal temperatures are occupational hazards for triathletes that should not be taken lightly.

Hyperthermia can kill you. Really.

The general rules are clear: take advantage of every opportunity during the race to drink and/or cool yourself. Don't think you can skip an aid station just to save a few seconds, because you can't. If you wait to drink until you feel thirst, you've waited too long. The trick is to *prevent* thirst.

Ironman etiquette: serve the water first as an appetizer, Gatorade as the entree, defizzed cola to clear the palate, and use a cold sponge for dessert. Never, never, spit your ice at a volunteer.

Perhaps staying hydrated—inside and out—deserves the most attention of all on race day. It's one of the things that race directors pay a lot of attention to at the finish line.

Signs that you are having trouble with the heat include goosefleshy skin, chills, light-headedness, and the inability to perspire. Another sign is disorientation—not good, because it takes away from your ability to gauge your own condition. This is the point at which triathletes must stop being endurance animals and start being smart. If you're unsure of your ability to make it to the finish line, don't try. It's no reflection on your ability or fortitude; it's a sign of your intelligence.

After the race, it's party time. Or maybe just quiet, cool-down time. Triathlons are fun and rewarding, but they can really take it out of you. It's a tough sport.

Just finishing a race can be a blast; forget the time, forget the place.

7
BUILDING A PROGRAM

On the following pages is a day-by-day training program designed for the novice triathlete. If you're a person with a strong background in any of the three sports, the word "novice" may be hard to swallow. If you've never done a triathlon, however, I'm not sure there's another word that fits. Bear with me.

This multilevel plan is designed to let you progress at a rate you're comfortable with. I've suggested a progression interval for each level, but it's only a suggestion. If Level 1 is too easy, move on. However, what's easy the first two or three days, or the first week, may not seem so easy in two weeks, so keep that in mind.

If you miss a day's workout at any level, skip the day completely and proceed as if you'd done it. Don't go back to try to make it up.

The system is broken into two-week clumps rather than weekly, and is designed to keep you running every other day. You can't run every other day on a weekly schedule; it all gets crimped on the weekend. Besides, weekly mileage

131

has gotten to be such a dangerous, addictive, egomaniacal thing. . . . ("I ran 150 miles last week," he said proudly, wincing as he moved. His knees were obviously shot. His cheeks were hollow and his eyes glassy. He hadn't shaved in several days, and there was a slight twitch at the corner of his right eye. He munched nervously on a carrot, then embarrassed all of us when he tried to shove a celery stalk in his mouth at the same time. "One hundred and fifty miles! In a week!")

I exaggerate, I admit, but not by as much as you might like to think. Stay as far away from the mileage obsession thing as you can. It's counterproductive. Some of the best short-distance triathletes in the world maintain a program of light, high-quality workouts in which the motivation and achievement factors are high and the breakdown factor low. Joanne Ernst became famous on a program like that; Kirsten Hanssen, the 1986 Bud Light USTS National Champion, thrived on a low-mileage schedule by necessity—she is one of the few top triathletes who trains around a full-time job.

The two-week format also works out nicely in that it gives you longish weeks alternately, first in swimming and cycling, then in running. Before moving on to the next level, always complete both weeks in the previous one. Then take a look at your training log, analyze your responses to the program, and step up.

The levels are designed with an international-distance triathlon in mind as a goal. On a steady diet of training at Level 4, you probably would be able to get through a longer race, but I don't recommend you try one in your first season of training and competition.

DAYS OFF

Several days off are noted on the schedule, and you should take them. But you also need to balance the need to be consistent and motivated with how your body feels. If you're tired—if you don't feel like training—then don't. *Listen to your body at all times.* Learn its language. If it's screaming for help, for rest—respond.

This is Harold Robinson of Ithaca, New York. It would be fair to say that he puts some effort into his racing, wouldn't it?

TAPERING BEFORE A TRIATHLON

Tapering, the process of reducing your level of training before a competition, is an inexact science at best. What works for one athlete does not always work for another—in fact, probably doesn't.

Try this formula for starters (Sunday race):

Monday and Tuesday—Normal schedule.

Wednesday—Cut normal distance 25 percent. No hard-paced work.

Thursday—Cut normal distance 50 percent. No hard-paced work.

Friday—Light jog (3 miles maximum). Light bike ride (5-10 miles, easy, low gears).

Saturday—Light bike ride (5 miles, easy).

Sunday—Good luck.

LEVEL 1: Base-Building Level 1

Goals:

1. Find the best way to fit a three-sport schedule into your everyday routine.
2. Gauge your fitness level and recovery time from one workout to the next. Be honest and realistic.
3. Establish confidence in the pool before you join an organized program.

Time requirements:
1½ hours a day, maximum.

Normal progression to next level:
4 weeks (2 repetitions).

WEEK 1

	Mon.	Tues.	Wed.	Thurs.	Fri.	Sat.	Sun.
swim	800 yd.	800 yd.	800 yd.	800 yd.	800 yd.		800 yd.
bike	10–15 mi.		10–15 mi.		10–15 mi.		10–15 mi.
run		3–5 mi.		3–5 mi.		3–5 mi.	

WEEK 2

	Mon.	Tues.	Wed.	Thurs.	Fri.	Sat.	Sun.
swim		800 yd.		800 yd.		800 yd.	
bike		10–15 mi.		10–15 mi.		10–15 mi.	
run					3–5 mi.		3–5 mi.

Notes:

A training schedule is much like a set of intervals in swimming: it seems easy at first, but at the end of the set you're dying. Stay at this level for the recommended month to see how the program works. If you don't feel sure that you're ready to move onto the next level, don't. Go another month with this one. There's no rush.

Be realistic about how much time you can put into your training. Keep travel to and from workouts in mind. The 1½-hour limit gives you time to shower and get changed at the pool, but there's not a lot of leeway. You might hear about being able to train for triathlons in an hour a day, but I don't think that's realistic.

Everything goes into your training log.

LEVEL 2: Base-Building Level 2

Goals:

1. Extend the limits of Level 1 gradually.
2. Fine-tune your training schedule with respect to your home and social life and your job requirements. You won't need to go far above the Level 2 distances to compete in a triathlon, so if you can make this work, things are going well.
3. Take a deep breath and join a swim team.
4. If you haven't done so, take another deep breath and pick a triathlon. Set a date between five and six months from your first day on Level 2.

Time requirements:
45 min.–1½ hours a day.
Normal progression to next level:
8 weeks (4 repetitions).

WEEK 1

	Mon.	Tues.	Wed.	Thurs.	Fri.	Sat.	Sun.
swim	1,200–1,500 yd.		1,200–1,500 yd.	1,200–1,500 yd.	1,200–1,500 yd.		1,200–1,500 yd.*
bike	15–25 mi.**		15–25 mi.		15–25 mi.		15–25 mi.
run		4–6 mi.		4–6 mi.		4–6 mi.	

WEEK 2

	Mon.	Tues.	Wed.	Thurs.	Fri.	Sat.	Sun.
swim		1,200–1,500 yd.		1,200–1,500 yd.		1,200–1,500 yd.	
bike		15–25 mi.		15–25 mi.		15–25 mi.	10 mi.***
run			4–6 mi.		4–6 mi.		4–6 mi.

*If you've joined an organized team, the number of yards you swim will likely vary from the figures above. Most Masters groups meet on weekdays, leaving you to fend for yourself on weekends. If this is the case, stick with the Level 2 schedule and use the opportunity to swim a steady, continuous 1,200–1,500 yards on Saturdays and Sundays.

**If you are riding indoors on a trainer, go two minutes for every mile on the schedule. Thirty minutes indoors, then, equates to a 15-mile ride.

***This is the first time a bike ride and a run are called for on the same day. Do one in the morning, one in the evening. I'd recommend the run first, then the bike ride. If you're comfortable at this level after 8 weeks—especially after the run/bike double, you're ready to move on.

LEVEL 3: Competitive Level 1

Goals:
Three months of steady work here and you shouldn't have a problem in your first international-distance race. Be consistent. Stay with the schedule. If things get easy, improve the quality of your work rather than increase the mileage.

Time requirements:
45 min. to 1 hour on your shortest day.
2 hours to 2½ hours on your longest weekday.
3 to 4 hours for long swim and bike in Week 1.
Normal progression to next level:
12 weeks.

WEEK 1

	Mon.	Tues.	Wed.	Thurs.	Fri.	Sat.	Sun.
swim	1,500 yd.	1,500 yd.	1,000 yd. (time trial)	1,500 yd.	1,500 yd.		1,500 yd.
bike	15–25 mi.	15–25 mi. (time trial)	15–25 mi.		15–25 mi.		30–40 mi.
run	1–2 mi.*			4–6 mi.		4–6 mi. (fartlek)	

WEEK 2

	Mon.	Tues.	Wed.	Thurs.	Fri.	Sat.	Sun.
swim	1,500 yd.	1,500 yd.		1,500 yd.		2,000–2,500 yd.	
bike		15–25 mi. (time trial)	15–25 mi.	15–25 mi.		15–25 mi.	10 mi.**
run	4–6 mi.		4–6 mi.	1–2 mi.*	4–6 mi.		8–10 mi.

*Jog easy directly after the bike ride.
**This is an easy bike ride that will help loosen up your legs after the long run. Conentrate on spinning in an extra-low gear. Keep your RPMs up around 85–90.

Notes:
Make careful note in your training log of any aches and pains. A little muscle soreness is normal, but any sharp pains that persist should be looked into.

The long run on Sunday of Week 2 goes back-to-back with a full day on Monday, Week 1. That's the reason for the change in your day off.

There are long bike rides and long swims at this Level. If possible, get the bike ride in early, then use the long, continuous swim to loosen up.

Work hard during the time trials, but don't go crazy. Concentrate on a firm, steady pace that you'll be able to repeat for comparison's sake. That way you'll have a good time.

LEVEL 4: Competitive Level 2

Goals:

1. You should be into a solid routine now, so begin to concentrate on several special days: the long days, and the multiple workout days that simulate what you'll be doing in a triathlon.
2. As you become a more serious triathlete, keep your training and the rest of your life in balance.
3. Run in at least one organized 10K a month.

Time requirements:
45 minutes is your shortest weekday.
3 hours is your longest weekday.

Normal progression to next level:
Stay here through at least one full season of competition.

WEEK 1

	Mon.	Tues.	Wed.	Thurs.	Fri.	Sat.	Sun.
swim	2,000+ yd.		2,000+ yd.		2,000+ yd.		2,000+ yd.
bike	15–25 mi.		15–25 mi.		15–25 mi.	15–25 mi.	40–50 mi.
run		4–6 mi.	1–2 mi.*	8–10 mi.		4–6 mi.*	

WEEK 2

	Mon.	Tues.	Wed.	Thurs.	Fri.	Sat.	Sun.
swim		1,000 yd. (time trial)		2,000+ yd.		2,500–3,000 yd.	
bike		15–25 mi.	15–25 mi.	15–25 mi.		30–40 mi.	10–15 mi.**
run	4–6 mi. (fartlek)		4–6 mi.	1–2 mi.	4–6 mi.		10–12 mi.***

*Run directly after your bike ride. Take a minute to drink something and maybe stretch a little before you head out.

**Bike ride after your run.

***Substitute a 10K when possible.

Notes:
Swims on weekends are long, continuous swims. Do them in the open water if the weather permits.

SAMPLE SWIM WORKOUTS

If you're not able to join an organized swim team or workout group, that doesn't mean you can't get into an interval program. Below are a few possibilities. Do each workout for a week so that you can get a feel for it, then shuffle them around for variety's sake—"A" on Monday, "B" on Tuesday, etc. Warmup and warmdown at a very slow, easy pace. "Moderate pace" swimming is strong, but not hard. Concentrate on technique.

You'll be able to push much harder—and you'll be much happier—if you can find a friend or two to train with. Barring that, a nonswimmer who can hold the stopwatch and encourage you can make a big difference.

How to arrive at a challenging interval:

1. Swim the distance hard. Don't sprint, but go faster than a moderate pace.
2. Add 20 seconds.
3. The first one or two swims on the resulting interval should be fairly easy, but you should get no more than 10 seconds rest. By the end of the set you should be working hard, but still be able to stop, look at the clock, take a deep breath, and go again. You will be surprised at how quickly you will begin to recover—and how long a silly little five seconds can be.
4. If you cannot hold the interval through the entire set, it is too difficult for you. Increase the interval by 10 seconds.

Note: Take a look at Joanne Ernst's training log in Chapter 3. Check her swim workout on 9/30. The 3 × 300 @ 4:00 set is a good indication of the kind of intervals we're talking about: approximately 10 seconds rest, and she's obviously working hard, since the next one is a little slower.

In the next set, the 3 × 300 @ 4:30, she is using the longer interval to increase the quality of each swim. Longer rest results in faster times and harder effort. This is a "quality interval," a variation on the interval theme often used for sharpening up prior to competitions.

1500-yard
A

X 200 w.u. (warmup)
> 4 × 75 mod. w/10 sec. (Four 75-yard swims, moderate pace with 10 seconds rest in between)
> 100 easy
> 8 × 100 @ 2:30 (Eight 100-yard swims on a 2½ minute interval)*
> 100 w.d. (warmdown)

1500-yard
B

X 200 w.u.
> 6 × 25 prog. w/10 sec. (Progressive—each one a little faster. Last one is hard effort)
> 50 easy
> 5 × 100 @ 2:30*
> 100 easy
> 2 × 200 @ 5:00*
> 100 w.d.

1500-yard
C

X 200 w.u.
> 6 × 25 prog. w/10 sec.
> 100 easy
> 4 × 200 @ 5:00*
> 50 easy
> 2 × 100 hard w/15 sec. (The difference in time between the two 100s in this set will be fairly large at first, but the difference will decrease as you get in better shape.)
> 100 w.d.

2000-yard *A*	*2000-yard* *B*
200 w.u.	200 w.u.
6 × 50 prog. w/10 sec.	4 × 50 @ 50 sec.
100 easy	50 easy
6 × 200 @ 5:00*	10 × 100 @ 2:00*
2 × 50 (One lap slow, second lap hard)	50 easy
	400 (Each 100 prog. faster)
100 w.d.	100 w.d.

2000-yard
C

X 200 w.u.
    25, 50, 100, 100, 50, 25, w/10 sec.
    10 × 75 @ 2:00*
    100 easy
    6 × 100 pull (Use a pull buoy)
    100 w.d.

2000-yard
D

200 w.u.
4 × 400 w/10 sec. (Moderate on the first one, then try to keep the others at the same time)
2 × 50 (One lap slow, second lap hard)
100 w.d.

*All these sets should be done at the correct interval for your ability and level of training. Keep track in your log book of what interval you were able to swim. Review your log before every workout.

Generally, you want to feel physically eager to go before a race, slightly restless over having done less than usual during the previous week. Err on the side of caution—it's better to go into a race too rested than not rested enough.

Whatever you do, don't change your diet or your normal daily routine before an event. The time to experiment has passed. Do what got you this far, what you feel most comfortable with. You'll be nervous enough on race day without having extra things to worry about.

The word is *taper*—right? Taper physically *and* mentally. Ease off. Have fun.

INDEX